Bits & Pieces

Of A Biologist's Journey into Spirit

A Powerful Extraordinary Continuous Healing Journey.

Janet Southall Connell

BALBOA.
PRESS

A DIVISION OF HAY HOUSE

Balboa Press books may be ordered through booksellers or by contacting:

Balboa Press
A Division of Hay House
1663 Liberty Drive
Bloomington, IN 47403
www.balboapress.com
1-(877) 407-4847

Because of the dynamic nature of the Internet, any web addresses or links contained in this book may have changed since publication and may no longer be valid. The views expressed in this work are solely those of the author and do not necessarily reflect the views of the publisher, and the publisher hereby disclaims any responsibility for them.

ISBN: 978-1-4525-4655-1 (sc)
ISBN: 978-1-4525-4653-7 (hc)
ISBN: 978-1-4525-4654-4 (e)

Library of Congress Control Number: 2012901804

The author of this book does not dispense medical advice or prescribe the use of any technique as a form of treatment for physical, emotional, or medical problems without the advice of a physician, either directly or indirectly. The intent of the author is only to offer information of a general nature to help you in your quest for emotional and spiritual well-being. In the event you use any of the information in this book for yourself, which is your constitutional right, the author and the publisher assume no responsibility for your actions.

Any people depicted in stock imagery provided by Thinkstock are models, and such images are being used for illustrative purposes only.
Certain stock imagery © Thinkstock.

Printed in the United States of America

Balboa Press rev. date: 4/11/2012

Preface

My life has been most challenging. There are many times I wondered how I survived it all. I was married to a man with multiple problems and we had a daughter with special challenges. We also had another daughter, our youngest; she is married and has children. While trying to handle family matters I was teaching high school biology. All of this was definitely demanding. Add to the mix working for a master's degree in counseling and getting certification at the master's level in biology while teaching school is, well, let's just say I learned much about living.

I am an explorer. I have always been interested in the extraordinary and always said prove it to me. Knock my socks off; well I got my socks knocked off. The little bit of information in the following pages is about bits and pieces of my life. I chose to write about some of the things that have survived in my memories. One particular incident was belief shattering. I have tried to explain it from my point of view. I think there have been some rather extraordinary occurrences. They have definitely caused me to rethink how I see and experience my world. I have had to adjust and include new ideas and concepts.

This actually has been a very exciting time to be living on the earth. There have been many rapid changes in my life time and I am looking to the future to see what comes next. I have read much trying to keep up with leading edge information especially when I was still teaching. There seems to be a huge volume of information in our world now. So much so that it is almost impossible to keep abreast of it all. We need synthesizers to research and then supply us with focused content. I must trust that what I need will find its way to me when I ask questions and want answers. You know when the student is ready the teacher appears. Just throwing a little information in here somewhere I read that the last twenty-five years from 1987 to 2012 the earth has been getting surges of cosmic energy, more than we usually receive. The surge of cosmic energy might explain some of the things that have been happening in recent years. This surge is happening because of our position in the universe.

It is my intention that the shared bits and pieces might help someone along their life path. Many people have touched my life and I certainly hope I can give back some of what I have received. Writing this has helped gel my ideas as well as put new concepts together. The ideas that were just rattling around in my head have found their way to these pages.

I think a pivotal point in my life was learning and experiencing the teachings of Ernest Holmes. His book "Science of Mind," is a philosophy, a faith, and a way of life. It just made sense and was so logical for healthy living: mentally, physically and spiritually.

And with that being said let's turn the page.

Blessings to you, Namaste, Janet Connell

A Recommended Idea

Or

How to Get Moving on Writing a Book

Back in the fall when I would share my story, the response would be you should write a book. I would tell the story again and the response was the same, write a book. Okay, what am I hearing here? Is the Universe trying to tell me something? Am I listening? Am I going to live what I am learning at this stage in my life which is living creatively aware? Write a book? Mmmm, that's an idea; I kind of thought about it and tucked it away mentally. All along thinking, who me, the nonexistent me, the non-valued me, who would want to read that. Those are self-esteemed thoughts of little value; got to change those thoughts! So, I would tell part of my story or comment about my ideas about life to a friend or family member in an e-mail then I would print out the page and slip it into my journal. That was the extent of my book writing saying to myself, I am saving printed stuff for a rainy day book.

Early one morning, just before stirring to get up, I was in what I call this day dreamy state. I love this place of consciousness; I think it's the alpha state, I think that's the creative state. It's a place I like to be, it's energizing, peaceful and where ideas flow. I had thought earlier in the summer that I loved being in this state. I was aware I have been there before in my life and wishing I could "call" it up more often. I always felt so much more peaceful and together after spending time there. I was able to solve problems without drama in this place of mind. Maybe the power of intent was at work. I was asking for more time in this place and I have received it. The Universe, the All that is, God is generous and abundant always telling us yes. We are the ones interfering with the yes.

One morning about a month and a half ago I was in this place of consciousness early in the morning. The ideas just started moving in, the name for the book and how it would manifest itself in bits and pieces of my life. I personally like short pieces of information and not long drawn out chapters of explanation. So, I got up out of bed. Turned on the computer and I started working. My fingers were bouncing all over the keys. Tap, tap, tap, ideas were filling the page. The sound of creation, my creation, this would be the story of my transformation, my paradigm shift. The story of how I have arrived at this point in my life. Everything was working to provide me with my current understanding of how things work. The ideas I am being acquainted with today are far better than the idea of being a lowly sinner worthy of nothing or a poor way fairing stranger or the person waiting to be rescued, you know saved from being a victim of life. The point is who is going to save me? I have been waiting forever. What a program to live life from? That was part of my old paradigm. But even that was useful as it taught me the opposite which is discovering who I really am, which is part of the Divine. I love me because God is love and I am part of God. The news is, God is ALL that is, and I am part of God, therefore I am a co-creator with the Divine. And I can't forget that everything is energy and everything is infinite. And it's a grand wonderful idea whose time has come. It is an idea of empowerment.

So, just maybe, could it possibly be, that some of the ideas I held to be absolute truths just might not be so! We might all need some personal paradigm shifts. Everything is part of God. Life is a work in progress to evolve man into a better more cooperative place on this lovely planet, Earth. The earth is a vibrant living system. It just might be experiencing too much negativity because of our belief systems. Those things we hold to be absolute truths, the things we are so willing to kill and maim others to prove ourselves correct. Why couldn't we just all go stand in the square and silently speak to our own personal God? Just let it be.

So this book is the result of ideas flowing into my head. Then I had to find a publisher. All of this happened so very quickly. For me when things just fall into place in such quick order, they are synchronistic happenings, and it means I am on the correct path. I have an intention. I am traveling from A to B and not exactly sure how I will get there. But I am quickly walking the yellow brick road and things are falling into place. Exciting events I can get passionate about when all seemingly comes together in such quick order. I discovered this publishing company the first part of November and now the first week in January I am almost ready to send this book in to be printed. Amazing!

Memories

Day 1

In the beginning there was nothing, a void, then there was the word of God saying let there be light and after 13 or so billion years there was Janet.

Day 2

For this life Janet came to planet Earth on October 14, 1943 arriving at 10:40 am in the labor/delivery at the old Mobile Infirmary close to five points where Springhill Ave and St Stevens Road intersect. It's no longer there.

Day 3

Her parents were glad to have her around they had been married for quite a while before she made her grand entrance. In fact her mother, was about to join the women's branch of the Army when she discovered she was pregnant.

All the rest of the days: My early days on Fulton Rd, I remember-

- One of my earliest memories was driving my tricycle under the edge of the house and trapping a finger. Ouch!

- I had a cat named Sandy; she climbed up a tree and got stuck up there. My dad had to retrieve her and the poor cat was so scared she pooped all over him. He was not happy. But the cat was out of the tree and I was happy.
- I remember my Mom washing clothes in the tub with a scrub board.
- Santa brought me a play house, it had the cutest little blue sofa and curtains over the two windows. On Christmas morning they kept asking me if I heard Santa building the little house. I was about four years old.
- I had an imaginary friend Zamby. Zamby did everything I didn't want to do. How was that for convenience?
- The gold fish freezing in the water bowl on the porch, they thawed out and were still swimming around.
- The floor furnace, with the grate, I used to talk to God through the floor furnace. It echoed back to me.
- We listened to the radio when the war ended; there was high excitement, elation, and celebration. I remember the emotion generated from the announcement. I was very young.
- I have a brother born on July 10, 1947. He cried all the time. Mother said he cried for the first fourteen months of his life or maybe it was eighteen months. And she used to sing "Pistol Packing Momma" to him.
- Going to the Loop Theater for a quarter and sitting on the floor if the movie got to scary.
- When I was in the third or fourth grade I went to town on the bus. I went all alone, what an adventure. I would eat at Kress, visit my aunt's dress shop and walk around down town like I knew what I was doing. I would have been about eight or nine years old.
- I went to Woodcock school for the first four grades. I danced in the May Day Court. I loved Ms. Harris (third and fourth grades) she read us the very best stories every day. I always looked forward to the new installment of "The Bobbsey Twin" series.

- I was in two Mardi Gras parades with the Loyal Order of Moose. My maternal grandfather was in the Moose. I rode once as an Indian maiden and then as a lovely spring beauty in an evening dress. This was when I was in the first and the fourth grade. I felt very important and special.
- I sang on the radio with the Mobile City Recreation Department.
- My Dad had a small gasoline powered racing car; it was a fun thing for him. He would run it in the driveway. It really was my brother's car but we all had fun.
- My mother sewed and made most of my clothes. I can remember her making my summer play clothes from flour sack material. The flour sacks of the day were colorful cotton prints that could be recycled into clothes.
- I don't remember this but was told; one day my mother got a call from a neighbor telling her to look out front, there I was about eighteen months old and I had disrobed and was prancing around in the nude. Oh my! The second time that happened I was probably in my forties and had run over a hornets nest while cutting the grass. I was covered up by agitated hornets and I was once again prancing around in my front yard disrobing as fast as possible trying to get them off of me. They delivered about 12 stings. Oh my again! A most painful oh my.
- I remember Irene, Tom, Cecilia, Marie, Hayes and Mark and Allen. Allen's mother was my kindergarten teacher, Ms. Sherman. I went to Ms. Sherman's kindergarten. It was on Duncan Street right off of Fulton Road at the Loop. I could easily walk to school.
- I spent the night with a neighbor one night and the roaches were all over the place. I can remember being fearful of sleeping and having the roaches climb all over me. I didn't want to hurt her feelings by not staying with her. Her mother was what I now would call abusive. She would beat her then lock her out of the house and she would scream and cry and beg to get back in.

- I remember getting sick at school, the measles or chicken pox and the elastic breaking in my underwear. All in the same day. Not a good day.

- I remember when my father, my brother and I had the chicken pox all at the same time. My father was very ill and the doctor visited the house to check on him. That was the day of house calls. My poor mother had to take care of us and we weren't that sick. We would jump up run around playing then hop back into bed and call for her to bring us things.

- We would go to my Aunt Mill's and Uncle Cooper's to watch TV. "I love Lucy" and "The Ed Sullivan Show" were our favorites.

- I had a very special aunt; she would pick me up on the way to her home on Fowl River. It was so beautiful down there, the river, camellias and huge old oak trees. She made me feel very special. I got to play with her jewelry. Wow, that in itself was a very loving gift. I have a special place in my heart for her. I got to sit at the big piano with her and we would sing, "Too-Ra-Loo-Ra-Loo-Ral (That's an Irish Lullaby)." That is one I remember. I got to play the baby grand too. I got to have a Coca Cola; she always said the whole word. And we usually would have delicious hamburgers and both of these were special treats as we never had hamburgers or Coca Colas at home. We had "real" food, vegetables, meat and milk at home.

- My mother was a great cook. She made the best yellow cake with penuche frosting. Today my brother and I search for "mama cakes." We have found one. Maybe?

Bits and Pieces

Or

Where to Begin

The Question: Where to begin? Where and when I start to think about my life it kind of all comes in at once like a woven tapestry that tells a story. You look and you can take in the whole story in a few viewings. They say a picture is worth a thousand words. But then when you settle down and start to really examine the pictures in the tapestry, you see the pieces parts. Since I have no woven tapestry, I will select words to describe my experiences. Sometimes when I have a project I see too much there and get stymied. I just need to focus on the pieces parts, the bits and pieces. One bit at a time. That's where the story is. We all have our story. Some of us just decide to tell our story. This has been an incredible journey of experiences. Well, here goes. But it's going to be in bits and pieces.

On the morning of Oct 14, I was ushered into this world at the Old Mobile Infirmary on Springhill Ave. During that time the mother had a tough time as she was to remain bed ridden for two weeks. I think that is just one of the many changes I have seen since the early forties. Today new mothers just about hop up off the birthing table and race home ready to proceed with the sweet new bundle. But, sometimes it's not so sweet, the midnight feedings, the early morning feedings and this tiny little bundle crying and you don't have a clue as to how to fix it. Oh my! I am responsible for this tiny little bundle that can only communicate by sleeping or crying. It can be kind of scary. And once we experience the change from woman to mother, we are never the same. Your life in an instant is dramatically changed. Oh wow, and that can definitely be overwhelming and quite a shock.

Becoming a mother is a huge change in one's life but what if there are problems such as a difficult birth, life threatening issues or abnormalities? These issues can take a toll on the family and its emotional health. I once read an article about life being like a journey and your destination was England. You planned for England your whole life. From experiences you had and ideas you had about England you knew what it was going to be like. Well on your way to England the vehicle suddenly switched direction and took you to China. Oh, reality sets in and China is totally different from England. Everything you thought was going to be has to be adjusted and your thinking has to change. Oh, if I had only known then what I know today. Some very fundamental spiritual principles would have been most valuable. Such as: Live in this moment! Accept what is! No judgments, just facts! Change my thoughts, change my world!

Well, the reason I have discovered those valuable spiritual principles is because of my journey and what it has taught me. I have had to reach and stretch to discover. It's all about experience; it's all about the journey. My intention is set, then the final destination is achieved but the journey is the experience, the teacher. We set intentions daily. Set your intention, and then set your mind on other things. Trust that your outcome will be what is desired. Ask and you shall receive. We never know when we start out at point A how we are going to arrive at point B. That is the magic in the journey. When we start trying to make it happen we miss the magic, and we also miss the mark. I knew none of this in the early part of my life I was just struggling trying to take care of the business of living.

We are always co-creating our lives but when we are aware we are able see the wonder and the magic in the journey as we move from point A to point B. James Redfield says tell your truth then look for synchronicity. For me synchronicity is the wonder and the magic. It's the Universe talking to me when it pulls things together. It's a tingly empowering thing.

Today it's easy for me to see the magic and wonder of the journey because of what I learned and what I know but the actual journey was emotionally challenging. My sanity demands that I see my life as a huge learning experience; I must see the positives and understand the spiritual significance.

Biological Life In A Nut Shell

Life is composed of 4 major compounds: Proteins (body structure)
Carbohydrates (fuels to run the body, plants)
Lipids (fats, oils and waxes)
Nucleic acids: DNA, RNA

DNA contains the coded message to: 1. Build a body
2. Maintain it
3. Send the code to the offspring in chromosomes.

The basic working machine in the body is the cell. It contains the nuts and bolts that make everything work. It performs the duties necessary for life to function. The cell is composed of protein and covered with a fat shield. The fat shield is necessary as we are 75 percent water. Water and fat don't mix. The fat allows a barrier between the environment and the cell.

DNA has the code that makes the proteins, the body parts. The cell membrane (barrier), the part that is exposed to the environment, allows certain molecules from the environment into the cell and if a protein is needed then the DNA is uncovered, unzipped and the coded message is revealed to make the needed protein. The RNA then reads the code goes about gathering up the pieces parts of the protein, the amino acids, and the protein is made; ready to be used as needed.

When a cell needs to reproduce in order for life to continue into the future the DNA is condensed into special structures called chromosomes. Condensed structures are much more easily managed when moved. Humans have 23 pairs or a total of 46 chromosomes. This is a good time to look at the chromosomes to determine if there are any irregularities such as Downs Syndrome or Prader-Willi Syndrome to name just a few. When the new cell with its 46 chromosomes is ready to work in the new environment the DNA then exits the condensed chromosome arrangement and stretches out into long strands that are easily read.

DNA is the master blue print for biological systems. The cell membrane reacts to its environment determining which protein is needed from the DNA. So in reality the cell's environment selects the needed protein, it becomes the controlling factor. The DNA follows the directions of the cell membrane and makes the protein.

DNA is a coded message that is based on only 4 molecules for simplicity, A, C, T and G. As these molecules are arranged in a liner strand the combination of letters dictates the building blocks for the body proteins. These 4 molecules are read in groups of 3.

This is simplicity in action. It usually takes about 100 building blocks (amino acids) to form a protein.

This would be a very small segment of a DNA molecule unzipped coding only for 4 amino acids. Just to give an idea of how it works.

For example: ACT would be the code for one amino acid, as would ATC, GTA, CAT, and so on. This would be what is read on the DNA molecule. Then RNA reads this code and goes out into the cell picking up amino acids and drops them off in the appropriate sequence for the appropriate protein. The sequence of amino acids determines the type of protein. This is the actual code, A, T, C and

G there is only 4 molecules to make *ALL* of life. How simplistic is this? Four little molecules and how they arrange themselves in differing patterns is the blueprint for all life here on earth. Wow! Yes, even including plants.

DNA is found in the center of the cell, the nucleus. The gathering of the amino acids is done in the rest of the cell's internal environment. Life is pretty amazing, all of life not just humans.

Well, of course, how could stories about my life not include a little science? Just one biology lesson, maybe even more than one. Smiling here, I have an audience, you. Lucky me, teachers need audiences.

DNA is the master blueprint for organisms. DNA has been on a roll it has just popped into our world in the fifties. Or rather let me say *we* have just discovered it and the escalation of understanding has been sweeping through science and the world. Of course it's always been there, if there is life there is DNA. Understanding DNA helps to explain some of the mystery of life. Just as other science concepts help to explain some of the mysteries of life. DNA is the master blueprint for these bodies we live in. Our bodies allow us to experience life here on earth, life in this dimension. We are consciousness; we are capable of being aware of our place in time and space.

Frogs

Or

A Teaching Story

Frogs have always been one of my most favorite animals. They are so adaptive. They can be found in most environments. Some of them can be buried up for years encased in a cocoon-like covering. When the rains come again they know and come out of the mud to reproduce and bury back again until the next rain. Most of their life is spent in the dried up earth encased in their cocoon.

I was driving to work one morning and spotted a "huge" bull frog on the side of the road. I put on the brakes, turned the car around on a dime and jumped out with my trusty Wal-Mart plastic bag. I covered the frog with the bag and he jumped. I missed! The second time, I was a winner I had scooped up two large bull frogs. Unfortunate for them I interrupted their mating dance. All I could think about was sharing these wonderful guys with my students. I kind of secured them at my feet. As I think back this was not such a safe thing to do. But I didn't want them jumping around in the back of my car. I am recalling the time I found an octopus on the beach. We put him into a jar of salt water and lightly placed the lid on the jar. We then put him on the floorboard on the passenger side. On the drive home he pushed the lid off, climbed out and attached to my mother's leg. This was the point when a little chaos erupted in the car. No kidding! Now, frogs hopping around my feet while driving wouldn't have been good idea. But, I got to school without an incident.

I carried my bag in and couldn't wait for teacher show and tell time. I put them in my store room in a big drum thinking they would be good there. I pulled them out first period and showed them to the students and we talked about frogs. After a few minutes I put them back into the drum. Next period I went back to get one and one had escaped. It had jumped out of that drum. The drum was waist high. I then went after the frog that was splatting around on the floor in my store room. Adventures come in all shapes and sizes. I caught up with the frog and showed her to my students, another show and tell. I returned her to the drum. How do I know it was a "her?" She was larger and didn't have the fat thumbs like the males. Anyway, I showed them off again. They were getting tired of performing for me and they started screaming like a child every time I went back there to get them. I was amazed. They were very stressed. They didn't realize they were to cooperate with me as a teacher show and tell activity. This was an Ah! moment for me I was totally unaware of the stress level of the frogs. I felt their panic. At the end of the day I returned the frogs to the swamp. They jumped away having given a day of their lives for the teacher and many students. What a great gift they gave us. I loved it.

There are frogs that carry babies in tiny little pouches on their backs. Another variety of frog holds the babies in their mouth. The Aborigines drink "frog water." When there is a drought they know where to find the buried frogs and then they squeeze them to drink the water they have reserved. Frogs of course go through metamorphosis as they change from eggs into tadpoles and then into frogs, they have a very unique life. Frogs are most adaptable and very interesting animals. If there are environmental problems frogs will be one of the first to respond as they are amphibious, having both water and land lives.

Maybe we have a parallel experience with the frogs as we are transformed at the end of our lives into another dimension. Life itself can be a transformation.

Snakes

Or

Those Things That Speak Fear

Nature is talking to us. The indigenous peoples have considered themselves a living part of the Universe, a part of their natural world. They communed with their world, which included the snakes. Up until the last few years I have considered myself *apart from* the Universe, in it but not of it. My consciousness was a little shifted out of place. Having studied the natural world professionally, as a biology teacher I was acting as an outside observer. I had a "eureka" moment a while back, how could I have been so unaware of being a unique part of the creation in this universe. Oh! My gosh, I am an active participant in the world, a product of it. I am still kind of in awe to have been so unaware, so removed from such a huge truth.

Some thirty plus years ago I saw this huge black snake hanging from a bird house in my carport. I am 5'1" I couldn't see in the hole of the house without standing on a step stool. He was hanging from the bird house to the floor in the carport with his head in the hole. I automatically reacted, shovel in hand and heart beating like a drum in a parade. I was ready, set, go to save the bird eggs (Not really sure I remember if there were any birds or eggs.) and remove the fearful animal. Who's fearful, of course me. I captured the snake with the shovel, terrified to lift the shovel fearing he would get away I scooted him from the concrete pad to the grass at least ten feet. Then I raised the shovel. The rest you can imagine. I remember being so overwhelmed with the fear. I was so amazed at how my body was responding after this all occurred. My body was telling me all about fear.

I heard a story the other day about a lady who just felt she needed to go to her backyard and check on her dogs before leaving the house. She saw a small snake on the path. Her fear was speaking to her; she grabbed the large hedge clippers and yes, you can imagine. I made a remark, "Oh, no, you didn't." She said yes she did. I am much more tolerant of snakes today than I was for the black snake in my carport. My fear is much less intense.

So: here come the snakes. Being in touch with one's world, listening, paying attention, trying to find a path that leads you, it's a new place every day. How do we listen? What are the clues? Do we have signs? Do we listen like the indigenous peoples? Are we aware? Does the universe communicate with us? I believe so in many different ways and in this instance the snake. The very next day after talking to the lady about her backyard snake I looked out my back door onto my patio. Yes, there was a snake about two feet from my door. He had to come from an entrance 14 feet away (it's enclosed) and up a step onto the actual raised patio. Woops, there's the fear taking to me. I got the broom and decided I was sweeping him away. I scared him as he pooped on my patio. I had to do some sweeping to get him out of there; he wanted to stay. Nope! I got him out into the backyard. He still wanted to head back for cover and I had to work to keep him headed away. He wound up in the drain that leads to a big holding pond. I hope he found his way. I have to say the exercise of removing the snake made me perspire, a by-product of the fear. He was a harmless garter snake. There are several little girls that play in the yards behind me. The snake had to go. And do you think that's the truth? He was camping out on a big girl's patio is more likely the true reason for the snake needing to go.

The next day I turn on the TV there it was: a show about snakes, I switched channels and there it was: a show about overcoming exaggerated fears, yes, fear of snakes. Well I had enough snakes for a few days. I do realize there are many snake symbols in our culture. So I decided to look up snakes. This is what I found:

Serpent is a word of Latin origin (from *serpens, serpentis* "something that creeps, snake")[1] that is commonly used in a specifically mythic or religious context, signifying a snake that is to be regarded not as a mundane natural phenomenon nor as an object of scientific zoology, but as the bearer of some potent symbolic value. Snakes have been associated with some of the oldest rituals known to humankind

The **serpent** is one of the oldest and most widespread mythological symbols. Considerable overlap exists in the symbolic values that serpents represent in various cultures. Some such overlap is due to the common historical ancestry of contemporary symbols. Much of the overlap, however, is traceable to the common biological characteristics of snakes.

In some instances, serpents serve as positive symbols with whom it is possible to identify or to sympathize; in other instances, serpents serve as negative symbols, representing opponents or antagonists of figures or principles with which it is possible to identify. Serpents also appear as ambivalent figures, neither wholly positive nor wholly negative in valence. An example of a serpent used as a positive symbol is Mucalinda, the king of snakes who shielded the Buddha from the elements as the Buddha sat in meditation. An example of a serpent used as a negative symbol is the snake that tempted Adam and Eve in the Garden of Eden, as described in the Book of Genesis.

Snakes have many meanings in our culture and mythology. The internet is just filled with much information about snakes.

The next day it turned rather cool. I think he was hunting for a place to snuggle. Not at my backdoor. I am not sure of the meaning, that is the personal meaning for me, but I was awash with snakes for a few days. I am thinking the meaning might have something to do with transformation. Snakes shed their skins and become new. What an interesting couple of days with the snakes and my fear reaction. I haven't seen any snakes outdoors or on TV since then.

Scissors

I have always had students asking for scissors. They would use then to cut pictures for posters or whatever their needs might be. The day the young man asked me for the scissors I didn't stop to ask why he needed them I just handed them to him. He walked to the back of the room and was slightly bent over, facing the back of the room. The young ladies sitting at the very back and facing forward had him in their line of vision. They were pointing to him like you've got to see what he is doing.

He turned around and walked to the front where I was and it seems he had taken the scissors and cut his pants along the seam line from mid-thigh to mid-thigh. He had actually cut along the crotch line of his pants. I was so astonished I think I kind of hollered at him, "What in the world did you do that for?"

He just kind of looked at me and I said come on let's go to the office. On the way down the stairs the science teacher below me saw us approaching, she was also rather amazed at what she saw. Of course this was most unusual not something one sees every day in a school.

It turned out he had wanted to go home so when he made the request and he had been denied he had devised a plan. Do something bizarre and then I will get to go home. Well, that is exactly what he was allowed to do. He was sent home for a few days.

I have since learned he was killed by someone while serving in the armed forces. I don't think it was in the line of duty. This young man had much against him if my memory serves me. His family life left much to be desired as his father was in prison.

I must say that this scissor classroom situation has remained in my memory all these years because it was so out of the ordinary.

As with so many students they have several strikes against them so early in their lives, it's an uphill struggle for some of them. We just can't find explanations for experiencing such challenged lives. But the earth provides us with many experiences to grow and evolve. The number of experiences that we are able to have here is infinite. It is my belief that we are spirit having earthly experiences, to teach us as we evolve life on this planet Earth. It's all about experiencing.

A Significant Event

Or

The Light Came On

My father was an electrical contractor and then he taught the electrical trade in the local trade school for many years. He was a smoker and I was too. To stop was the issue. He was diagnosed with a brain lesion around '85. So, during this time the issue of stopping smoking came up. We teamed up and he and I took a behavioral modification class to stop smoking. We did some things like wear a rubber band on our wrist and pop it when we wanted a cigarette. We also were directed to collect up old cigarette butts and put them in a glass jar and fill it with water and let it sit a few days. Now if that doesn't evoke a picture of nasty, ew, it was pretty stinky.

Well, it didn't work because he was smoking very close to the time of his transformation in '88. It didn't work for me either. I struggled with stopping. I tried silly tricks to stop. I would leave my cigarettes in the car and the intent was to leave them there. Down pouring rain: here I was with my umbrella going to the car to retrieve the nasty little things. I even tried hypnosis and I was so busy watching the process of hypnosis I really don't think it worked. Anyway I didn't quit smoking. Since then I have been hypnotized and I believe I can tell the difference compared to the first time. I did start taking tai chi around '91. I thought maybe that would help.

Smoking was really pretty nasty. I coughed a lot and it really made me feel kind of yuck. It really stinks and smoking puts yourself at risk as well as the people around you. It is a difficult drug to quit and definitely a very bad habit, it's an addiction. I was tied to them and really didn't realize how much until I finally quit and didn't need to be sure I had cigarettes and a lighter no matter where I was. It's like a child and his blankee. It was obsessive compulsive, I couldn't go anywhere without them.

So how did I quit? The night of August 12, 1992 the ceiling light came on in the middle of the night. At the time I was still married and asked my husband if he had turned it on. Being awakened with a bright light in the middle of the night is startling just like a little electrical shock. I took it as my father speaking to me, my omen was to stop smoking. I never struggled and I just never lit another cigarette. So that's how I quit smoking. It was a noteworthy moment.

I was aware of a shift in my consciousness as if one minute I was a smoker and the next I wasn't. I can remember the changed view, it is difficult to describe but it was like here today, gone tomorrow. What a blessing. I am so grateful.

The Time Line of Experiences

Or

Things Aren't Always as They Seem

Early on in my relationship with my ex-husband he was diagnosed with

Ankylosing spondylitis (Marie-Strumpell Disease). The spine fuses. He was given the diagnosis that he would be wheel chair bound by the time he was thirty. That didn't happen. It is my understanding it's an autoimmune disorder.

Shortly thereafter was the birth of our mentally challenged child. She had a very difficult time getting here and came into this world face first, which is considered a breech birth. At the time this type of birth was believed to have caused her slow developmental problems, or that was the prevailing diagnosis. Today we know it as Prader-Willi Syndrome. She had some other little things like a crooked foot. It was straightened by the Orthopedist over a period of time. Molding and reshaping the foot every week with plaster casts allowed the foot to be straightened. This is easily done over a period of time when the bones are still soft and pliable. She also had tubes in her ears for reoccurring ear infections and she had an extra footplate muscle in her eye that caused it to pull inward. That muscle was clipped and the eyes were straightened. Things went rather okay, well, to say, at least challenging. Especially challenging as I was mentally questioning the reasons for this situation. Self-blame is of no value. I gave it much energy. Remember it's like preparing for a trip to England all your life and then the train is diverted to China. Adjust, Adjust.

Then in February 1979 my husband had a total hip replacement in his right hip.

The hurricane season came the year of 1979. On the gulf coast we are very aware of this weather disturbance that can appear during the fall months. Frederick made its appearance aiming for the area of the coast where I live. It was definitely something I had never encountered before, well at least not to that magnitude. I spent the night in my mother's basement with my head covered with a pillow trying to mask the sound of the wind blowing. It was most frightening. It sounded like a freight train running through the house all night. I went out the next morning to survey the area and the leaves from the trees looked as if they had been ground up and sprayed on everything. Trees were down and there were limbs everywhere. The insects were so angry; I was walking down the street and was popped by something, wow! That sent me for a whirl. My parents lost their house at the beach; there was nothing but a couple of sticks left. It was shocking to see what had looked normal the day before had been totally destroyed. The environment was totally changed. My house on a small canal had seven pine trees on the roof. It was absolutely a huge mess as pine trees were down everywhere. Many had been snapped off about half way up the trunk of the tree, leaving toothpick trees with no tops. It's unbelievable the amount of energy that's contained in a hurricane. The energy is transferred to the areas it passes through. It looked like a war zone. The earth has some powerful forces.

We were two weeks without electricity, up at dawn to bed at dusk, using candles and cooking on a grill. We had the only phone on our street, imagine that. I was outside all day cutting, moving, stacking, doing the grunt work of clearing debris. It was rather strange that I felt very alive and energized after physically working every day and I was outside in nature. Ding, Ding. A clue here, for being in nature, being active and feeling energized and feeling very alive. We had to have a new roof and while cutting a broken tree it fell into my dining room wall so that had to be rebuilt. Oh yes, I now think "do I want a mini vacation or stay and experience another hurricane?" I'm no dummy; I didn't have to get the book for dummies on how to avoid hurricanes. Is there even a choice, I opt for mini vacations.

Then one December day after Frederick, I was shopping at the local market. I saw my sister-in-law running across the parking lot at me waving her hands and looking rather urgent. There were no cell phones then. She was delivering a message to me that my husband had taken a fall and I needed to come at once. When I got there everything seemed to be in the emergency mode. It was definitely *not* one of the best days of my life. He had been helping my brother cut a tree, one of the toothpick trees. While the truck was pulling on the tree, my husband was cutting it. All at once the tree split and he was thrown about fifty to seventy five feet from the base of the tree. When I saw what had happened I went into an emotional frenzied state. I was like the ant that had its ant hill stirred with a stick. My youngest daughter stayed with him and held his hand. I was flitting around trying to call the paramedics, they had already been called. I was in a state of shock. As I write this I am re-experiencing the emotional trauma of the situation.

It was my ex-husband's birthday. He had broken the femur in his right leg below where the hip was replaced. The hip was totally fine, that was amazing. He had also broken his neck, C-1, the first cervical vertebrae. He wasn't paralyzed or dead because the vertebrae spread out into three pieces when it fractured. Because of this it hadn't constricted the spinal cord. C-1 is a very important spot for the spinal cord. All of the body below that point would not function again if severed and that includes breathing. His head was also dislocated about three centimeters. The doctor said he had never seen this type of fracture on a living person. They placed him

27

in a halo, an apparatus which screws into your skull and is attached to braces on a vest which is worn over the chest. The purpose is to immobilize the head and hold it in a straight line thus giving the C-1 a chance to mend. He wore the halo until May 1980. The leg was reluctant to heal; it was in a cast with pins running through it and the cast was for immobilization. The leg was not healing; this was three months after the accident. The doctor said let's put you in a body cast, within two weeks he showed remarkable bone formation at the break site. I think it took until May to heal. He was in the hospital from December 15 until February. Then every time he had to go back for imaging or testing or to the doctor we had to go in an ambulance. He couldn't fit into a car he had too many restrictors. I was trying to work and be the caretaker, whew!

Following this there was another hip replaced. He popped them out on occasion and we had to get an ambulance to take him to the hospital to sedate him and manually pop them back into place. On one of these occasions they discovered his heart was compromised. They found blocked arteries and they did a triple bypass. He had a recovery time and things were just regular for a while.

He had a spider bite or something on is foot. The tissue on his foot had eroded down to where you could see the tendons. Ew! They were searching for a blocked artery in his leg restricting blood flow to the wound. Blood flow enhances healing. He was very bent over because of the disease and wearing the halo for so long. They determined his posture had caused his major aorta from the heart to collapse and it was restricting his blood flow. They proceeded to go in and replace it with an artificial aorta. The anesthetist was intubating him and poked a hole in his throat. His tissues were filled with the anesthesia gasses and his head and neck were dramatically swollen. It was shocking to see. After a month the throat healed and the major aorta was replaced with an artificial one that wouldn't collapse. At the same time they put an artificial artery down the leg to the affected foot.

He still went to the hyperbaric chamber several days a week for about a year for healing the wound on the foot. In the meantime they tried to sew up the place on the foot. Unknown to me they tried to connect with his spine to deaden him from the waist down to work on sewing up the wound in the foot. They tried five times to enter the spinal column. His spine was fused. My opinion: *horrible* procedure! Finally they used local anesthesia and sewed up the wound only to have it tear open about four days later. This all happened within the last four months of 1996. Oh my word! And in our culture, not being gender biased here (smiling), men aren't good patients but then women aren't always good patients. This was a very trying time. His life was so challenged. All of our lives were challenged.

He was now the bionic man, who was probably in the best health he had ever been in. But I might add he was still smoking. Perhaps I had a delayed reaction to all that had happened. I just thought I was going to die if I wasn't removed from the situation. One of the most difficult decisions I have ever made was "do I stay in this situation?" "Or do I leave this man with all these health issues and a mentally challenged daughter?" In late 1999 a year after I retired I finally got enough courage to tell him I just couldn't do "this" any more. It was all very painful. I had so much grief, I guess in my mind it boiled down to them or me. I chose me. When someone asked me "Do you want to live the rest of your life the way you had been living the first half?" That was the decision maker. My daughter stayed with him. I am sure she was very confused and she wanted to stay in her nest, something that was familiar. He was petrified of being alone. Even though I wasn't there on a day to day basis I was still having her on weekends and he was still depending on me for help. In the eight years after I left, he had to have a few simple surgical procedures. I was the one there.

During the following nine years I was able to travel. It was truly a gift. I was feeling alive again.

When hurricane Katrina came on shore we were no longer married. He had five feet of water in his house. It was pretty much a huge mess. It was an emotionally trying time. Honestly it was really horrible. I was reminded of the first half of my life. I was there helping.

Somewhere during all of this, I think the eighties, I was going over the moon bridge at a garden in my area and I slipped and sat on my ankle. It was very painful and my foot was a little wobbly when trying to stand up. As it turned out it was broken. This was the first weekend of summer vacation and I spent the rest of the summer confined and walking on crutches. I discovered the delicate nature of moving a cup of tea from the microwave to the sofa. One of my students came and helped me master the tea cup. I did master the solid objects with a nail apron I had gotten from the hardware store.

Through all of this I was there, overwhelmed, teaching school and just trying to keep my emotional earth legs. How can anyone endure such health issues? I kept observing and have come to my place of understanding today. I believe that you will understand my philosophy from what I have written throughout this book. His life gave me much understanding about life. It was very, very challenging. Care-giver is not at the top of my list of things done well. I have asked myself many times what have these life lessons taught me? What was the purpose for such a challenge filled life? My answer changes with my level of understanding concepts and ideas about life and living.

It is my belief some of us live out our presence on earth being victims. We are all victims at one time or another. There is a payoff in every role we play. To be a victim we must be able to see that role played out or live that role and then understand the opposite which is personal responsibility. Being personally responsible means we are the creators of our lives with our thoughts, our ideas and our actions. Personal responsibility means I am responsible for all I do, all I say and all I think. How I behave and react to what's in my life belongs solely to me and no one else. I look within. My job is to discover the spiritual laws by experiencing them. Then I can make a contribution to the human race and its consciousness. Just one part of God at a time makes the whole world a better place. I am reminded of the song "We are the world."

I have come to believe that we are all here to learn, as teachers and as students sometimes reversing roles. We are _ALL_ part of God, everything, even to infinity. I believe we are all interacting to learn about life. My understanding is that we are spirit having earthly experiences. I have been learning the spiritual laws of the universe and helping evolve life on planet earth as I evolve. I have been in earth school learning lessons of forgiveness, love and trust; these concepts I learn by experiencing the opposites. This is why things aren't always as they seem.

The "Beatitudes" stated here.
Blessed are:
The poor in spirit: for theirs is the kingdom of heaven.
They that mourn: for they shall be comforted.
The meek: for they shall inherit the earth.
They which do hunger and thirst after righteousness: for they shall be filled.
The merciful: for they shall obtain mercy.
The pure in heart: for they shall see God.
The peacemakers: for they shall be called the children of God.

This is an excellent explanation of living and experiencing opposites here on earth. I really understand the Beatitudes today. I can't say that has always been so. This was told to us long ago. How can we arrive at the final destination without first knowing the opposite? We receive a gift of knowing from experiencing opposites. Sometimes things aren't always as they seem.

Mother Theresa

Or

An Incident I Found to Be Strange

During one of my very trying times when I was experiencing much anxiety I tried many different things to quiet the anxiety. I had purchased a book about healing. There was a procedure that you were to do several times a day. This consisted of positioning the fingertips at specified points on and about the face, head and neck. While the hands were in place you were to recite a little saying 6 times and then move to the next position. I believe there were about 6 positions. I think it's an energy clearing procedure. Well, I did this several times a day for a few days and oh my I was feeling not better but way worse. I was feeling like I was going to expand and explode especially in the area of my brain. I decided this wasn't working for me and stopped it. Sometimes we will try most anything, especially if it's noninvasive, hoping to discover a break in the clouds. It's a measure of miserable. Misery is an inertia buster (explained later). The question would be: How miserable was I? What would I be willing to do?

I just decided I had enough of this particular technique and turned my attention to something else. My father had done rehab work on fire jobs early in his electrical contracting career and he had come across some crystals from an old chandelier. They had stayed in his desk. He made his transition in 1988. When my mother made her transition in 2003 they were still in his desk drawer. I kept them. I tied a string on one several years ago and hung it in my kitchen window to catch the light as it came through. It formed rainbows all over my kitchen walls. I love the pure colors and I like to think of them as being magical. In the early nineties I started painting pictures because I thought playing with the colors would be fun. It turned out to be a great stress releasing tool.

So, I looked and found the other crystal and proceeded to tie a string through the hole in the crystal pear drop. I wanted more crystals in my window for more rainbows. I tied the string. I then held the string to get ready to put it in the window and the crystal began to spin so fast that it was a blur. It kept spinning. I was thinking this is so weird. So I held the crystal and let the string dangle downward. It had wound so tightly it had kinks up and down the string. I proceeded to smooth out the kinks in the string, making it straight. Once again I held the string and placed the crystal hanging down. It started spinning again at a super rate of speed. So fast I could hardly distinguish the object as a pear shaped crystal. It was a blur. Now, for some reason I just decided to command it to stop spinning. It started slowing down and I made another command to stop and it stopped. Wow! I was thinking what is going on here? My immediate thought "I don't want this kind of power." All I could see was me as Mother Theresa serving others in the cardboard shanties in India. That was not for me. I would also have to be *so mindful* of my words. The words I still struggle with especially when I drive.

Much of my life had been caregiving. I am not that good at caregiving. Or rather let me say I would rather think I had other attributes. I am still trying to determine what was happening. I just kind of throw it into the "pot" of other experiences I have had that I can't explain. It's an energy thing. My best guess. That's a very broad answer. I am an explorer. Yes, it was a little strange. I interpreted it, strange and an energy something. Just sayin.

Indiscriminate Drug Use

I had several episodes where I thought I was going to die; I was thinking I was having a heart attack. This was after my divorce which was in 2000. This would have been around 2004-5. I drove myself to the emergency room two different times, one year then the next. I did some cardiac studies at that time. They noted no problem, after the second time I got a note telling me about anxiety. No one ever mentioned anything about anxiety. I remember thinking it was like "we don't discuss this," probably because we don't understand it. It's like the elephant under the rug. So since we don't really understand much other than what we observe with our 5 senses, and can measure with our current technology, we try to treat the symptoms with a drug. The current paradigm: a health complaint, we get a drug, and then another drug to fix that symptom, then another drug and so it goes. At this time of my scare I was given a script for Prozac, I took it for about a month until I was traveling about seventy five on the interstate and totally turned my car around crossing from one side of the road to the other in three lanes of four o'clock traffic. I missed all the other cars and the concrete barrier in the center of the road, what a trip that was! My heart never skipped a beat, nor did my body react to the fear, I am thinking this is so "not-normal." So I gradually stopped taking the drug because it also made me very uncomfortable. These anxiety episodes were showing up about once a year usually around my birthday. I didn't think that was often enough to take this drug. What was I thinking, the words in my head about aging, they were bubbling up to the surface and speaking to my body. *Emotions give us many clues that allow us to look and see what we might be able to change to evolve and grow.* When drugs block the emotions we don't have the opportunities to grow.

When my ex-husband made his transition 2008, I was very distressed because I was the only one responsible for my mentally challenged daughter. Before that time it was a shared responsibility. I was experiencing so much more anxiety so I went to the walk-in clinic one day and I was talking ninety miles a minute explaining all and of course she picked up on the anxiety. I'm sure she was thinking: this lady is a classic case of anxiety let me give her something for this. She is so wired. Let's help her, so I got a script for Lexapro. We can only function from our level of understanding at any given point in time. As Jesus said Father forgive them for they know not what they do. Forgiveness is always the case, when we know better we do better.

Let me say here my belief about drugs is something I picked up from my mother. That is drugs aren't good for me, they affect me adversely. She had many reactions to drugs and she lived until three days before her ninetieth birthday without taking drugs. I watched her after bypass surgery sit in a stupor for several months and she kept saying the drug is doing this it's killing me. Finally one day I guess she decided this is enough and stopped taking the drugs that the doctor had insisted she take. From that point on she improved dramatically. She had an aunt that also experienced drug reactions. So back to the Lexapro, I was given a month's supply. I was really rather reluctant to take them. But I was feeling so weird I decided to try them. I took the first one and oh my, I thought I was dying! I drove myself to the emergency room. The next day the internist told me to take half the dose. I did for a week but then I decided this was kind of okay so I tried the full amount again with the same reaction. Again, I was back to the emergency room totally whacked out. The only person who really talked to me was a male nurse. He told me he thought I was reacting to the drug and would be okay when it wore off. They sedated me I was in never never land. When

I was recovering from my reaction this second time I said no more Lexapro. That was it for me and Lexapro. I did find something that worked, Xanax. Everyone was so wary telling me how addicting it was. But it worked! And I didn't feel weird. I have taken them when needed and I certainly am not addicted.

Perhaps my belief system about drugs was the creating force behind my reaction. But I am finding that many people are having adverse reactions to many drugs. Perhaps they just treat the symptoms and not the cause. Maybe we need to have another look at what are the causes of disease. Some we know such as bacterial and viral infections but many are not known. Some causes just might be energy disturbances of the body. Everything is energy, Einstein told us this. If our bodies are contaminated with negative energy then we might have some symptoms that can't be treated with drugs. This idea will be explained a little later in the bits. I think we are on the leading edge of incorporating new discoveries and ideas about what causes dis-ease and what dis-ease really is. There might be a problem as we have some lag time here between new information and its introduction into society. So treating the cause and not the symptoms maybe something we have to take responsibility for and not give our power over to the medical establishment. That is walking into the doctor's office and saying fix me. Drugs are treating symptoms not addressing the causes. I think that at least ninety percent of our bodies dis-ease is due to stress. The constant repeated patterns we do over and over again are based on how and what we think. The words we think become realized in our bodies. We must listen to ourselves. Be aware. What words are we using to describe our inner and outer world? Our emotions help us figure out the issue. Change the stinking thinking!

I have a vision that has a large office or a strip mall where there is a chiropractor, a counselor, a nutritional consultant, an intuitive health coach, an exercise program, a massage therapist, a meditation program, an acupuncture therapist, an energy practitioner and an intuitive/medium. We must include a doctor. I can't possibly forget the dentist. Smiling for those who know my brother is a dentist and I forgot to add this discipline and thought oh gosh, got to go back and insert this so I did. A new paradigm in health care would be how to address being healthy without drugs and using successful alternative modalities. Sometimes drugs are needed but not the way they are currently being dished out. I think there already are some places like this. But they are not in my area. If we are taking personal responsibility for our actions, our health and our well-being we will be out there searching for these healing modalities to help us fix the "in here."

The Agony of Anxiety

Or

The Search for Answers for a Better Life

Anxiety is a pretty miserable experience. It can be defined as nervousness or agitation, often about something that is going to happen and a subject or concern that causes worry. Another place I found: anxiety is a noun meaning distress or uneasiness of mind caused by fear of danger or misfortune.

So there you have it, all you need to know about anxiety, until you experience it. In which case you will stretch and stretch some more and go down paths you never thought you would travel trying to make it go away.

The symptoms: cold chills, feeling coldness in the heart center, feeling light headed, dizzy, feeling wrong, different, foreign, odd, strange, tingling, nausea, numbness, racing heart, trembling, shaking, and free floating fear just to name a few. For me the fear was of everything. When I was having anxiety my body responded in very strange ways. My digestive system went awry. It was scary. My blood pressure also went sky high. I had a physician tell me not to take my blood pressure when I was having a panic attack that it would just cause me more panic. In the current medical paradigm I would have been overdosed on drugs treating the symptoms.

It was a dark miserable experience. I was even thinking at one time it was Post Traumatic Stress Disorder. When we are exposed to stressors, the same unhealthy behavioral patterns over and over for a long period of time, the residual effects make themselves known. It's our body's response to the negativity we garnered over the long period of time and it speaks to us as illness. Many times I have experienced so much input from my environment I didn't have time to be the "observer." It can be overwhelming. I was overwhelmed. There were several times in the middle of the night I called Science of Mind and Unity prayer line for help to get through an episode. This has been since December 2008. It's just a very crazy place of being. I had a friend come stay with me for a few days after the second Lexapro experience.

I found it difficult to pinpoint the trigger for my anxiety. I just know that it was getting progressively worse. I felt on edge much of the time, almost like I was experiencing excessive energy. Then somehow I would go into overload and the anxiety/panic would show its head. Many a time it would happen just as I was trying to relax and go to bed. I would feel the strangeness and have to hop up out of the bed. I spent many sleepless nights. Sometimes early in the morning I would have to get up and walk. On several occasions I made a circuit through my house, walking the same path over and over again. I kept saying oh, this energy, it has to go.

I had watched someone in my area around the mall where I shopped. She would be out and about all day walking and pushing a baby stroller. I would see her everywhere in the area. Once I was close to her and she was in a rant just delivering a talk to someone that wasn't there. What I heard was rantings about the government, perhaps at one point in time she had worked for the government and knew how dysfunctional it was and was just spewing forth about it. I would think of her and would be fearful of winding up in that circumstance. Oh no, I would say, I don't want to live like this. My silent blessings go to her.

I tried music, I tried exercise, I tried chakra clearing meditations, I started going to the Science of Mind Church, I did tai chi, and I tried deep breathing exercises and counseling. I tried medication, the least effective cure as it put me in the hospital thinking I was dying. I joined an online group just for anxiety. There I found many people that had the same reaction to the drugs like I had. I read. I was searching. It was my intention that I was going to live the rest of my life in a more peaceful state. Anxiety wasn't blissful.

I tried these two people; I was flipping through the channels one night and found a man of religion talking. Call us and we will send you some holy water. He convinced me I got the letter and it said I was going to be experiencing unbelievable things I had never experienced before and it gave me directions on what to do with the water. They suggested a donation amount and I sent a donation. Well, this became a send us more money and we will send you more things. The second person I tried was an astrologer from online, she operated the same way but she told me that my summer months of 2011 were going to be extremely difficult to traverse. Because of the way they handled their finances I dismissed them both but I can't help but recall their predictions. This was two of the many paths I took trying to find the answers to resolve the anxiety/panic.

I do know it has been proven scientifically that water can be affected by negative and positive attitudes, thoughts. Dr. Masaru Emoto's work has given us evidence to support this. Water is an amazing compound with seemingly magical properties. It's only magical if we don't understand water's properties. The earth is the water planet and we are water bodies and the proportions are close to being identical. What about this Holy Water? I think it must be so! The earth is about seventy five percent water and have our negative thoughts affected the water? The earth is truly a living energetic system.

I must say I learned much about anxiety/panic disorder. It changed my life and part of this anxiety experience helped to totally rearrange my belief system. I am now confident there is much more to experience and understand than we can see with our five senses. It's amazing. I will elaborate on this in the coming "bits."

The Day The World Went Weird

Or

Other Ways to Communicate

I had a house phone with two satellite extensions. They both had only two numbers programmed into them. Both numbers belonged to my daughter, her home and her cell. I had used the programmed numbers for over a year without a problem. Then all of a sudden one day I tried to call one of the programmed numbers and got a strange recorded message. A strange man's voice answered and it sounded like he said my last name and that he would be sure that Connell got the message. Well, wasn't that strange. I dialed it again in fact several times and that's what the message sounded like each time. So I tried the other programmed number. It was correct and I reached my daughter. Then I tried the other programmed extension phone and got my daughter with both numbers. I didn't have time to sleuth the problem as I had to be somewhere at a specific time. When I returned home I started trying to figure out the problem. I was looking at the programmed numbers and discovered the culprit was the last 2 digits of the wrong number had been transposed. If it had been 75 it was now 57. I fixed the issue. The phone then continued to work just fine as it did before. This was after my ex-husband had made his transition, probably sometime in 2009. He had worked for the phone company and had a knack for electronics.

I had other things happen with the phone company, not sure if they were just happenings or what? I had a charge appear on my bill for a service I didn't have. The phone guy was to come about another problem with a phone jack that had been working very well. He was to come on Thursday he showed up the following Tuesday as if that was his day to come. By then I had already addressed the issue. All of these things happened in a short period of time, it was one phone problem after another. Then I moved.

I have a rock with the word *harmony* sitting on my windowsill in my kitchen. It is tilted back and leaning against the window. Just before all of the following occurred I awoke one morning to find the rock face down. It would have to have some fancy maneuvering to wind up face down without some assistance. The rock had been given to me by my ex-husband.

The most challenging day: I know why the people left the refrigerator for me when I moved into the house. It had already been fixed just shortly after I moved in. I woke up about a month later to find the original problem that was supposed to be fixed reoccurring. It was broken again. I made a call to the appliance guy and went on about my day. Then a little later I discovered my phone quit working, then my computer and my TV. So I was using my cell to phone the cable company. While I was talking to the cable company my cell went dead. My, oh my, nothing was working. The world of electrons was going, going gone. I went to get a new phone battery. The guy said the battery looked like it had exploded, at least now I had some technology that was working. I got home and decided to take a walk. I went to the refrigerator in the garage to get a bottle of water and it had stopped working. The food in that refrigerator had to be tossed. Now, I was thinking what is happening here and I was beginning to get a little stressed over all the outages.

I settled into the evening thinking things were on the up and up with the refrigerator repairman set to come the next morning. I was concerned about what to do about a refrigerator. I did discover that the garage refrigerator was on a plug that tripped. And I just reset the plug and the refrigerator started working.

Later that evening I was on the phone and I heard this horrible noise in my kitchen. My immediate vision was someone was in there with a metal rack swinging it around banging up everything. My heart started racing. Was there someone in my kitchen? I live in a relatively secure neighborhood. I dropped the phone and took off for the kitchen. The refrigerator was spitting ice out of the dispenser onto the tile floor. That was the noise. I was grabbing towels and trying to get the thing to stop. Somehow it did stop. I got it cleaned up and I thought all was okay. No, it wasn't done yet. It began again; it spit the rest of the ice cubes onto the floor. I was beginning to pray over this refrigerator. It was scaring me. I was thinking something evil was at hand. I took the container that held the ice out of the refrigerator. Thinking that would take care of it all. The refrigerator then kind of began to moan and groan and the metal bracket that turned the rod that pushed the ice through the door began to turn. I had removed the ice holding dispenser at this point so all I could see was the bracket. That's when I decided to just unplug this refrigerator.

The next morning I called the appliance man and told him not to come fix that refrigerator as it was going to refrigerator heaven. And I told him about the ice incident. He said he had never heard of anything like that before. As I recall all of this I can laugh but at the time I was thinking, gosh, I am totally crazy. It was stressful.

Okay, the next day I thought I needed an escape from the day before. I went to Biloxi where there are casinos. I do like to play the machines. Well, can you imagine my surprise when I won enough money to buy a new refrigerator?

I think there were too many things happening that day for all of this to be just a coincidence.

Something else, one day I was turning onto the interstate when all of a sudden my radio changed stations I had done nothing. The song on the new station was blaring "I got along without you before

I met you gonna get along without you now." I must say the new music amused me. Was the universe talking to me or was it my ex? This was when I was struggling over an issue about unrequited love. It was painful, not fun.

One of the reasons I am telling these stories is I feel it's evidence for much more than we can experience with our 5 senses. I am coming from a science background and that's where we must have facts. Just the facts, ma'am. Perhaps all of this is just happenings but they have a bit of strange about them, actually a lot of strange. I believe he, my ex-husband was communicating with me. I understand that electronics is a means through which the other side can communicate. Maybe it takes a lot to get my attention. Maybe he wanted me to know he was around.

Also during this time I discovered my lap top was behaving badly. It would cascade and wouldn't stop. I took it to a computer repair shop. The guy said it was working great he saw no problems. So I took it home and it began to do the same thing again, cascade. I took it to another place to run a diagnostic on it, no problem they could find. This happened another time, same diagnostic, same answer, no problem. I was feeling a little foolish. It's working fine now. Once again my ex-husband was very into computers. He also had this intensity about him to solve problems; he wouldn't stop until he was satisfied that the problem was solved.

One more story: A sensitive man, George Lugo, had a call on his cell phone; it was from an old friend. The old friend was saying he wanted him to call his father and tell him where some important papers were located. George then called his old friend's father. The father answered the phone and George proceeded to give him the message about the important papers. Then the father asked how he knew this information and George said he had just talked to his old friend, the son on his cell phone. The father was rather shaken up as was George because the father told him the son had made his transition to the other side several months ago.

Anecdotal evidence is valuable when it begins to bubble up into our reality with regularity. Hopefully science will try to explain what is happening and not just dismiss it as insane. We are governed by the laws of math, physics, and chemistry. These are real stories that have happened to people. Another story: a man received an email from a close friend who had made his transition six months earlier, it said I'm watching. We can dismiss these incidences or take a second look to try and understand them. We can call them crazy, which is a judgment. Judgments aren't peace makers, what they actually do is push people away.

A Life Changing Story

I might preface this with the fact that I have been very interested in science and spirituality. It has been my focus now consciously for about 5 years but in actuality since I started studying to be a biology teacher way back in the "olden" days. I also believe that I am a spirit having an earth experience. Einstein told us everything is energy. Since we know energy can't be destroyed then the word death needs to be removed from our language and transformed needs to replace it. There is a measurable difference when the body is left behind and the spirit moves on. And quantum physics allows us to take a peek through the door of how some of it works. I think when we have dramatic emotion filled experiences with another we build a large energy field of entanglement. You know telepathy and that connectedness feeling we get with certain people. I believe what we focus on with intention and emotion from the heart (another way to say prayer) becomes part of our reality.

This is a thought I had after this experience which I am about to tell you. I had been driving around with a flyer on the front seat of my car for about a month about a "Radical Forgiveness" workshop. I think I had set an unconscious intention to help resolve the anxiety/panic I had been experiencing. It had been especially troubling since Dec 2008. I tried drugs and I had reactions so trying to get through the anxiety without drugs was the issue. Only one worked Xanax. As I said I have done many modalities: prayer, music, relaxation, meditation and even consciously committing to a spiritual path trying to resolve the panic. Before 2008 I would have anxious periods about every year or so and even farther apart than that. I had a hugely challenged life and recently I was thinking I had PTSD (post traumatic stress disorder). I was having some of the symptoms.

I had been thinking about past life regression as of late wondering if I explored that topic it might help me find a more peaceful place from the anxiety. I was searching for answers to understand the nature of this beast, anxiety. I was thinking perhaps it was a past life. I was wondering if my current life with my ex-husband was left over karmic resolution from lives lived before this one. Before I continue, I think we (all of us) have been here many times, many life times. Questions we ask will be answered when the time is right and I was asking many questions. Also, during this time I was thinking that I could have helped my ex-husband make his transition simpler and easier. He was petrified of dying. But, in 2008 I didn't know what I know today. With all I have experienced in the last few years, oh, wow. The electromagnetic anomalies these last several years: the phone issues, the many TV issues I haven't mentioned, the refrigerator issues, the computer issues there were many things that just didn't have a rational explanation. I hadn't had these kinds of issues all clustered together before in my life. I think life is a continuous unfolding awareness. When we are ready to see we will see. When the student is ready the teacher appears.

So, this is what happened: I went to a small gathering the evening of August 12, 2011 with an intuitive/medium, Teresa Brown. There were 3 of us along with her. She was wondering why her group was so limited and after our meeting she said the experience confirmed her questioning the smallness of the group. I think it was a little more than what she usually experiences.

So she began with a prayer of protection asking the Father to protect us from any harm. She was asking us to ask question, I asked her about my life path and she said I was on target. I told her my interested in science and spirituality, and that science explained life and life has spiritual qualities. I said science especially physics enhances our understanding. Then somehow we got around to an ex-husband question. I made a remark about having a very challenging life for so many years living with him. He was not especially sweet. She then said he was in the room with us and that he had gotten stuck and couldn't make it toward the light. I was so startled; at this point she definitely had my attention. He had been there hanging around me since he passed on December 2008. When she said that the other two women confirmed picking up on his energy, we were all having goose bumps (a spiritual confirmation). One of them said her legs were feeling so weak and heavy and her lower torso was responding, feeling very heavy. This is not surprising considering his depressed energy. The other lady experiences spirit with her heart as it begins to flutter. There are no heart problems as she has been checked out. Her heart was fluttering indicating he was there in the room with us. He had stayed Teresa said because I was a comfort and was familiar to him and he didn't know what to do (He was stuck in a familiar pattern, my opinion). She said he was almost like a, and she paused looking for a word then she said, savant and that if he had been born thirty years later his path would have been much easier. She even mentioned genetics, that genetics was responsible for his difficult life here. He once told me he thought he was responsible for our daughter's problems and when he told me that it was almost like his soul talking to me. I then told Teresa about all the strange electromagnetic anomalies I had been experiencing and how he was brilliant with electronics but he had huge emotional issues. She said he was definitely here with me and had been trying to communicate through the electronics. Everything she said just seemed to click with me. She asked was there anything I wanted to tell him. Popping into my head I said forgiveness for all of the trauma. Remember, I had been driving this radical forgiveness poster around for a month. There was a lit candle on the table and she told me to put my hands together and pass them over the candle first one way then turn them over and pass over it again. She explained this was a forgiveness ritual for clearing negative energy. She began the ritual with the blessings of the Father, Son and Holy Spirit. (She is writing a book about the importance of rituals in our culture.) She asked if we might send him to the light with his angel. The light was where he needed to go to receive purification after living this life. (His presences here on earth, had because of the density of his experiences, become clogged with impurities, negative energy. The light allows us to see within [what we did while here] and purify our energy. The light is total acceptance, pure love. My opinion.) She said he was crying because of all the pain and suffering and forgiveness. Poor guy his life was so compromised. This was a very emotional moment the tears were blurring our vision and wetting our cheeks. It was all very emotional and still is when I get to this part of the story. She then said a prayer holding the candle and in the name of the Father, Son, and Holy Spirit, she then got up and went to the door opening it for him to leave along with his angel and go to the light. I really felt a little silly doing this but I was paying attention and I was doing whatever she said. It was a very dignified loving exit. She also told me this lifetime was wiping out a lot of our karma from the past. This confirms my "past life" questions. She told me my life should be considerably different. But the next few days would be, well I found them a little emotional. I was adjusting to this new very unusual experience. The next day, Saturday, August 13, 2011, she told me I should celebrate my new found freedom because he was/had been holding on to me with all he could muster for a very long time even before his transition. I took my daughter to lunch that Saturday. Today, I can confirm my life has a new found freedom.

Now for the biggest thing of all: I feel lighter and the anxiety/panic is gone. *How glorious is that!* I am so filled with gratitude. Actually I had a few little residual uncomfortable periods and went back to see Teresa about a month or two later. She said my energy field was extended out too far and she showed me how to bring it in. At the time she did some energy clearing on me. I didn't understand nor can I even explain this other than my old reliable statement. We are energy. But what I do know is I am good. The anxiety /panic is gone and drugs were not the correct answer. I am so grateful because it really was a very difficult experience: that fear. Whew! Pretty scary stuff. It was awful.

I am thinking (my opinion) I am no longer connected to his heavy depressive dark energy. I was experiencing what he did, even when he was living as our energy fields merged because we were married with many strong emotions. There was quantum entanglement. Now, if I was picking up on his fear when he was here and then when he reached the other side he was in a very bad place. I was in a very bad place with my anxiety/panic. I think he had no idea what to do so he clung to me for comfort and solace. I was picking up his "stuff," wow, if so he was totally miserable. It was scary. But what a tremendous thing he did for me as he allowed me to see a glimpse of the other side. I totally believe all I have written in this book. This was a total life changing experience for me. I think my life has done a 360 degree shift. I am so filled with gratitude that I am aware of what I know this day because of this experience. Things aren't always what they seem. This all seems pretty weird. Yes! I definitely think so. It has made me think, think, think.

I might add I go to a NDE (near death experience) group once a month and have been now for several years. This has been an interest of mine for many years. They all experience seeing the light and then returning to life to live out their lives here on earth. They are no longer fearful of death because they have been to the other side and come back to tell about it. In the past many people were hospitalized for relaying their NDE stories. Society thought them to be crazy, how absurd!

She, the intuitive/medium said I should write a book. This is about the fifth person that has told me this. So this is my story in bits and pieces.

Hope I haven't totally wigged you out and it makes some sense. This is my explanation of what was going on. The fact was he was still here, but on the other side and I was experiencing this very scary anxiety/panic disorder. And then he left and the anxiety left.

51

So of course the who, what, when, where and why went to work. And this is my explanation. And some would say, just say yes to the new state of consciousness and that's it. Instead I am writing about it. Because things aren't always as they seem. If this can help anyone understand anxiety/panic then I have accomplished my goal. I might ask a question here and that is:

"Why are we treating anxiety/panic with drugs when it just might be an energy issue?"

What about other so called mental health issues we are treating with drugs? And we discover the drugs don't work, that should be a clue. Could it be there is a crack in their reality that is allowing them to experience otherworldly energies? How would we be able to communicate this to anyone based on our current paradigm? You would be saying I feel like I am going crazy. And in reality you really would be experiencing someone's energy. You wouldn't be crazy at all. When the energy was removed the healing occurred.

We really don't die we are energy and it's transformed to another dimension. As Jesus said in my father's house there are many mansions. I consider death nothing more than just a transition to another place.

I do know that when Teresa allowed me to realize my ex-husband was still around me I was kind of totally just being in the moment and listening to this experience. It was totally new and different and so irregular in nature for me. I was just listening, and being aware to see what would happen. And I was a little wary. As I said I went back to see her again about two months later and she said my energy field was too open. If I was sensing his energy then just maybe I could sense others too. Perhaps that was a factor in my anxiety I was too open picking up too much stuff. I was opening psychically but totally unaware. Everyday I pull in my energy. Salt is a purifying agent and I sometimes use a salt scrub when I shower after being around many people. There are seven billion of us, that's a lot people, that's a lot of positive and negative energy. I do know that I am no longer having anxiety and I am having sleep filled nights, a true blessing. Now and then I might still be awake at 2 am, but most of the time sleeping. Yes! I am so filled with gratitude because this anxiety experience is over it was no fun at all. It was a driving force for me to seek relief from the emotional pain, as I was searching for answers. It was an *inertia buster*. I am no longer having the anxiety. It's like the storm has blown away. Oh, WOW! This knocked my socks off. And this is now four months later and I am so good. And my paradigm has shifted drastically. Science and spirituality! Yes, there is definitely a connection.

Energy, everything is energy vibrating at different frequencies allowing different experiences. I have been so blessed to have had this happen because in the end it was a gift. I just "know!" Maybe as the mystics say there are no miracles, it's the workings of the universe, the All that is, God, and it's a little explainable if you kind of understand a little of the mystery. We, us humans have developed science to help explain how things work. Science is discovery it is a means to understand life and the universe. We are co-creators: Spirit residing here in these earthly bodies bringing spiritual understanding into this earthly existence. It is my opinion we are part of God, we are here and God is all that is. So that makes me and you part of God. All of us! At least to my reckoning as we evolve and grow.

Random Energy Experiences

Or

Wired or Weird

Okay, I am so hooked on energy, after all everything is energy. Have I not told you so, many times thus far? Some random experiences over the years have snagged my attention. They struck me as not the ordinary happenings we are programmed to accept in our society. I had tucked them away for a later understanding. Today I can say I think they are energy happenings. I believe if I had to categorize them, well, I am not so sure I can, but I can tell you what I think they might be.

Also, before I divulge some of these occurrences, I made a vision board. A vision board can be a poster with many added pictures that give a visualization of what you want created in your future. We are creating our reality through experiences all the time. First we have a thought, and then we set an intention. We see it happening, we can visualization it and then it becomes reality. My vision board has several things on it but one corner has a large picture of Abraham Lincoln with a big headline saying knowledge, in fact that whole corner probably twenty-five percent of the board is suggesting knowledge as the topic. I have been learning so much new information. I am internalizing all of it rapidly and sometimes it's so fast and so much that I feel a little confused trying to put it all together. I have to rearrange my mental constructs to include this information. Just because I am older doesn't mean I stop learning. Thank goodness, I have a passion for learning, but not just anything. Actually I am in the process of answering questions I have been asking all along about life. Something happens, I don't understand it and I will ask why and how and will eventually get an answer. Some of the questions I may have asked twenty five plus years ago.

I might also add here I think that my questionings about life landed me in the spot I find myself today. My biology degree in teaching was answering many of these questions I had about life, those who, what, why, where and when questions. My traditional university degree was the foundation for the understandings I currently have about life on this earth. Life is pretty wondrous.

I have several of these isolated what I call energy incidences, so let me begin with the first one that stands out in my mind. Sometime ago probably when I was in my early thirties I read there was this metaphysical (meta means beyond) phenomena one could do to make clouds dissipate. So I went outside and focused my attention on a *tiny* cloud. I mentally focused on the cloud to dissipate. To my amazement after a small amount of time I noticed the cloud began to disappear. I was so amazed, surprised, that this actually occurred I thought I had to have many trials with the same result for verification. So I have done this countless times since then and every time I get the same result. Today they dissipate a little quicker than they used to. Okie dokie, now what's happening here and what does this mean? All I can say, there was mental focus for the cloud to dissipate and it did. I couldn't explain it. To satisfy myself I decided that thoughts were energy and they were projected out to something with a command. And the matter followed suit. Okay, is this significant? Does this mean all thoughts are energy, and when projected with focus something happens? What would we call prayer? A thought projected asking for a result.

One summer I took parasitology and genetics working toward my degree. I had children then I got my degree. I was doing everything, meaning all the family things and I was so mentally and physically stressed. I was feeling I had no control over anything in my life and in the middle of the night I saw this light. It was consciousness, not an electric light, I was in the presence of this light and it was total peace. I don't know how long it lasted. I just remember seeing and experiencing this awesome light.

In another incident I was quietly sitting in the tub one night trying to relax after a day of teaching. I put my hands together as if I was praying palm to palm, finger to finger. All of a sudden I could feel this taffy like pull if I just pulled my hands apart only slightly and I was very focused on what my hands were doing. If I slowly very slightly adjusted my hands apart and then back together without actually touching, the feeling expanded. I decided to try it out of the tub just standing on the ground. I could do it but the feeling was lessened. Then I tried doing the same thing again sitting in the bath tub and concentrating on my breathing, I was focused, taking deeper breaths and more relaxed. I also did something mentally like going up and over. Like an upside down J with the top of the J at my upper back and the curve of the J going up and over kind of in my mid brain dropping down just behind my eyes. That's the best I can describe it. Are you totally confused? Each of these activities caused the sticky taffy feel to increase in between my hands. My body energy and my hands were completing the circuit? I don't know, just somehow energy. There are many modalities of healing hands maybe that's what it was. But it's still energy and I was feeling it and aware of what increased it. Those who meditate have been telling us how important breath is. Focused breath makes a difference.

Then there is the electric blanket. Electrical currents are moving through the wires in the blanket. I had a blanket some years ago and felt it then. But because society encourages us to throw out such nonsense notions I just kind of thought okay. If I told this story people listened but didn't respond much, just smiling here. Oh well, I can guess what they were thinking. Part of the problem then and now is to trust me. But now I am more aware and am beginning to trust that these are real incidences of experiencing energy in our world. I did read a study once in the past about humans resonating with the frequency vibrations of electricity coming into their homes. The changed frequency in Europe also produces the same results. I just recently tried using an electric blanket again. I really like the light weight of the electric blanket and the warmth it provided, but it made my body pulse. The more relaxed I was the more able I was to feel this pulsing. It was feeling "not normal" so I hopped out of bed and pulled the plug. No pulsing. Now I am wondering if it is okay to experience this electricity so close to one's body. I understand there have been studies of health related issues for people living close to the high voltage power lines.

When I quit smoking it was because of the electric light coming on in the middle of the night. I didn't turn it on. But I quit smoking. There were all those other things that happened. Were they energy things, electrical things? They were strange things. I don't know.

Within the last year when I would reach to turn off a light it would blow the bulb. Quite often this happens. In fact this week it happened and my watch battery went out the same day. I got a new battery and it's out again. I also have had a couple of times when I would reach out to touch someone and the sparks would fly and this would be during the summer when static electricity isn't so prevalent. I actually saw the sparks between the fingers. This past summer in a very humid warm environment every time I would touch my car I would get shocked. Energy, energy.

Not long ago I was sitting in a chair and someone walked behind me. As they walked by I was so dizzied that I felt I was going to fall out of my chair. It was definitely coming from the person's passing; it was like a sweeping effect I could feel his energy field or something swirling. I have again felt this from another person just the other day. I decided it was their energy field and I was receptive to it. Is that psychically aware? I have no idea I am just exploring.

Sometimes when I am in bed almost asleep, I suspect I am in the Alpha brain wave state. There are four brain wave patterns;

energetically they are as follows in order of frequency. Beta, very mentally active place, then Alpha the dreamy place, then Theta deep sleep, then Delta very deep sleep unconscious, like with anesthesia. So on with the almost asleep state. I can "see" it's like behind my eyes these wheels of color like an old 78 rpm record that are flexibly spinning and spiraling upward. The colors are usually dark magentas and purple. The coloring is almost like a tie-died t-shirt. I think this has something to do with the energy centers in the body, the chakras.

I am throwing in a little blip about the Alpha brain wave state. Sometimes I find myself in the almost awake and almost asleep place where I am exploring. It's like I am in the land of ideas. I get up not wanting to forget what I was picking up on so I immediately come to the computer and begin to type. I mentioned this in the "bit" about writing the book. I love this *place* it has such a great feeling about it. I call it a place but its consciousness; it's a very creative place or state of mind. I have no idea what to call it. I am not sure I can access this place at will, somehow I just find it. I personally believe that Einstein spent much time here as did many of our creative geniuses that have given us so many new ideas about our natural world. They helped to build the knowledge base of our world as we know it today. I have heard it said the information is all here we just must discover it, and then become aware of how it adds to what we already know. We have to throw out and readjust pervious ideas to make things workable. I read somewhere when all four brain wave states are working simultaneous we are mentally expanded to cosmic consciousness. Is this enlightenment? I have no idea just asking. I think this would take much practice.

Okay another thing; if I focus on the sky just kind of looking at nothing but everything I can "see" little burst of lights. They are all over the place everywhere actually looking like tiny little photons popping around. They are kind of shaped like little mini comets just everywhere you look. I don't think they are in my eyes, I think they are out there because I can sometimes see the veins pulsing behind my eyes if I focus on it.

Several years ago when magnets were the going hot item I bought a magnet pad for the bed. It kept me awake all night. I boxed it up and sent it back. Not sure what was going on.

Our gathering of information is not always from outside ourselves but within as we react and interact in our world of energy. The experiences are very subtle. I suspect there is much more. I think we have been programmed in our current society to only validate using out five senses and anything unusual just can't be so, it's denied. Fear also plays a role, the fear of anything different or unusual or new. And when we fear we respond with the fight or flight response either attacking or running away. Perhaps we need to find a middle road and replace our flight or fight response. Can we even replace this response? After all we are no longer on the savannah, no more mastodons or saber tooth tigers to get ready to defend ourselves against. Fight or flight might just be an obsolete human need, but we are still using it. It's the fear, it creates havoc with our body chemistry and I suspect our energy fields. What are the fears we imagine today? The fears are giving us clues about what we need to address in our lives.

The Body's Energy System

Or

Information I Borrowed From the Internet

I found this information to be very informative and easily understood. It is a good explanation of the energy systems of our bodies. In 1939 there was a process developed called Kirlian photography. It is defined: The process of photographing an object by exposing film in a dark room to the light that results from electronic and ionic interactions caused by placing the object in an intense electric field. The photograph shows a light, glowing band surrounding the outline of the object.

Dr. Thelma Moss of UCLA devoted much time and energy to the study of Kirlian photography when she led the parapsychology laboratory there in the 1970's. The photos of objects show a bright field or edge just around the object. If the object had a focused prayer or thought sent to it with love the bright field or edge would be expanded. I found this to be most interesting. I was aware of this research in the late seventies. Does this prove thought is energetic?

I have had something called an aura photograph made recently. It was of my upper torso and I was surrounded with deep green merging to deep blue then to deep purple expanding outward. There were 3 circular distortions in the colors just above my head. They gave me an explanation and I found it to be most interesting, He said that he had not seen an aura like mine. He described it as showing a higher frequency development than many he had observed. What does this mean? I have been working on spirituality and that was an indicator of accomplishment? I am not sure what it meant. The man making the statements was an engineer by profession but had retired and become involved with aura photography. He said the three circular distortions were my guides, my angels. I think they say the colors denote a teacher and a healer. I had another one made several years ago and it was totally different as it was yellow and green with a touch of blue. Both of them were lovely, I love colors and like being surprised by the results and hearing the explanation. The images are always different. It's a fun thing to do. I have read the aura constantly changes with emotions and thoughts which are always influencing our energy field. Some people can see auras but thus far I haven't been able to naturally see them. I am not sure what this is all about, but it was interesting. I loved seeing the brilliant colors surrounding my torso. I am relating the above information to the following concepts I obtained from the internet when I googled body energy systems. The information appears here as I discovered it on the internet. I had read about the energy body systems back in the seventies and early eighties. I felt this information was straight forward and easily understood.

The Sanskrit word "*chakra*" means literally "spinning wheel". The chakra system within the human body consists of seven major chakras and many minor chakras. To those who can see energy fields, a major chakra resembles a spinning wheel when looking directly into the chakra. However, viewed from the side, it looks more like an energy vortex somewhat resembling the shape of a tornado. This energy funnel is tight and compact near the surface of the skin, and gradually widens as it extends outside the physical body to the outer edge of the aura.

Each major chakra from the Root through Brow has four energy vortices associated with it: one spiraling upward, one downward toward the earth, one out the front of the body, and one out through the back of the body. The upward projecting vortex from one chakra and the downward projecting vortex of the chakra just above it join to form an energy column that runs vertically through the physical body from the bottom of the spine (Root Chakra) up in front of the spine and out through the top of the head (Crown Chakra). The Crown Chakra has two vortices, one opening upward toward the heavens, and one projecting downward into the energy column running through the body.

When a chakra is "healthy and balanced" its front and rear vortices spin in a circular motion. However, if there is a disturbance or blockage in the flow of energy within a chakra, the circular motion may become elliptical or, in extreme cases, severely flattened on its sides. This distortion may be sensed by those able to see or feel energy fields, or indirectly sensed by a pendulum. Further, each chakra has its own specific "frequency" or rate of spin, with the lowest rate of spin in the Root Chakra, and steadily increasing up to the highest rate of spin in the Crown Chakra.

The purpose or function of the human chakra system is to take in higher-dimensional energy from the Universal Energy Field all around us and translate or step down its frequency of vibration to that which can be used within the physical body. Each major chakra vibrates or spins at a different rate, and each chakra will absorb energy from the UEF that is harmonically related to its own frequency. Thus, energy from several frequency bands within the UEF is absorbed by the different chakras and is directed by the internal energy meridians to those organs with which that chakra is associated:

Energy Bodies

The five-layer *Energy Body* system is the third way of describing the Human Energy Field. Note that the physical body is counted as an energy body since all matter is ultimately made up of energy. Also of importance is the fact that the higher subtle energy bodies overlap and interpenetrate the complete physical body. In much the same way as many different TV signals exist around us in the same space simultaneously and can be individually identified by a specific frequency, the overlapping subtle energy bodies (which are also defined by different frequencies) also penetrate into the same space as our physical body. So when an energy practitioner places his or her hands on the client, the healing energies are sent not only to the physical body, but also to each higher energetic body. Thus, with the proper healing frequencies channeled through the practitioner, healing can occur on not only the physical level, but also in the etheric, emotional, mental and spiritual energy bodies of the client.

The Physical Energy Body. At first, it may seem unusual to consider that the physical body is an energy body, but that is exactly what it appears to be. And as we explore and become more accustomed to this new paradigm, we are able not only to see the physical body in a greater, more meaningful context, but also we begin to understand the role of disease and the nature of healing. The physical body is the densest form of energy that our consciousness uses to explore its environment and interact with others. By the densest form, it is meant that the vibrational patterns of the physical body are of a frequency low enough to be seen by our eyes (they are within the spectrum of visible light), heard by our ears (about 30 to 15,000 Hertz), and experienced with the senses of touch, taste and smell which are within the "frequency capability" of our physical body.

But there are many octaves, frequencies, and vibrations beyond the capability of our physical senses. Beyond what we can see as visible light are the higher frequencies of ultraviolet, x-ray, and cosmic radiation. We are beginning to understand that what we can physically sense is only a small portion of the vibrational energies around us. And if we look within our physical bodies at our atoms, molecules and cells, again we find patterns of vibrating energy that we have traditionally called "matter".

We need to become aware that our physical body is really a field of vibrating energy that has coalesced from higher less dense octaves. But we also need to remember that as vibrating fields interact with each other, one field can affect another field through the phenomenon of sympathetic vibration. If a violin player produces a note an octave above Middle C, and a second violin lying nearby on a table has a string which is tuned to Middle C, the second violin string tuned to Middle C will sympathetically begin to vibrate as well. So as we also begin to understand that there are several vibrational fields of energy around our physical body, it becomes easier to understand how one field affects another through this principle. And this is the key to understanding how energy-based healing techniques can achieve such visible and profound results in the physical body.

The Etheric Energy Body. The etheric body is the first energy body in frequency above the physical body. It exists within the physical body, and extends outward about an inch outside the skin of the physical body. Its purpose is to form an energy template or matrix for the development, maintenance and repair of the physical body. The etheric body contains a vibrational energy counterpart for each organ, blood vessel and bone found in the physical body. Indeed, the etheric body contains the energetic blueprint for the pathways that guide the location and development of every cell of the physical body. Our physical bodies exist only because of the vital (etheric) field behind them. This etheric field exists prior to, not a result of, the physical body.

Since the etheric body is the physical body's blueprint, the two are very closely related. The energetic vibrations of the etheric body determine the pattern for not only the physical tissues and organs, but also the state of health of those tissues and organs. If the vibrations are not clear and pure, this disharmony will be reflected in the physical body as disharmonious function—what we call "disease".

Conversely, traumas to the physical body (e.g., broken bones, burns, incisions and scars) will in time be reflected into the etheric body unless there is some interceding process that either prevents this reflection into the etheric body or which restores the original vibrational pattern which existed prior to the trauma. The ability to work with a client's vibrating energy fields is precisely what forms the basis for rapid and effective energy-based physical healings.

An illness can appear in the energy field weeks and even months before it appears in the physical body. In his book, *Vibrational Medicine*, Dr. Richard Gerber, a Detroit physician, notes that "The etheric body is a holographic energy template that guides the growth and development of the physical body."

The following description of the etheric and higher subtle energy bodies surrounding the physical body are taken from Barbara Brennan's book, *Hands of Light*. To her, the etheric body appears as a grid of tiny energy lines which has the overall structure and shape of the physical body. This matrix extends from 1/4" to 2 inches beyond the physical body. It is upon this etheric grid or matrix that the cells and tissues of the body develop and are anchored. The etheric body appears as a light blue or gray matrix of lines of light that constantly pulsate or scintillate at a rate of from 15-20 cycles per minute.

The Emotional Energy Body. The emotional body contains the emotional patterns, feelings, and vibrations that determine our personality, and also how we feel about ourselves and interact with others. If we are constantly angry, always feel helpless, or are consistently fearful, these patterns or vibrations get locked in our emotional energy field and become a part of our personality. This determines to a very large degree how we interact with others on personal, social, and cultural levels.

The emotional body generally follows the shape of the physical and etheric bodies, but is somewhat more amorphous and fluid, and extends from one to about three inches outside the physical body. It contains energy "blobs" of all colors of the rainbow, depending on the specific feeling or emotion. Highly charged feelings such as love, hate, joy, and anger are associated with energy blobs that are bright and clear, while confused feelings are darker and muddier.

The Mental Energy Body. The mental body contains the structure and patterns of all the thoughts and belief systems that we consider as true. And there is a very strong connection between the mental and emotional bodies. Although a thought or idea can in itself be very powerful, our reactions to those thoughts carry even more energy, and different people will react differently to the same thought.

For example, consider the thought form "If you are not a Catholic (or Protestant, or Muslim, or Jew, or whatever), you can not go to Heaven." One person might hear that thought or idea, think it was silly, and give it absolutely no energy. But another person might become very passionate, depending on his greater belief systems, and argue strongly either for or against the truth of that statement. His emotional body would then record the intensity of the reaction to the thought stored in the mental body. However, the person who thought the statement was silly in the first place would not have any resonance with it, and no energetic pattern would be stored in either the mental or emotional bodies.

The mental body usually appears as yellow light radiating around the entire body from head to toe, and extends from three to eight inches beyond the physical body. Within this area, individual thought forms appear as small blobs of light of varying form and intensity.

The Spiritual Energy Body. The spiritual body (i.e., all vibrational patterns in octaves higher than the mental body) contains all the information related to our experiences, and reflects our gestalt consciousness of all that has been learned and experienced. It contains our higher intentions, our sense of what is right and wrong ("conscience"), and our desires to increase our awareness of our purpose, place and mission for this lifetime.

These five energy bodies make up one's Human Energy Field, or aura. Its outer shape appears roughly egg-shaped and extends out to perhaps 1½ to two feet beyond the physical body; however, this shape can be extended even further out or contracted closer to the physical body depending on the situation the person is experiencing. For example, when a person is feeling emotions of unconditional love, the aura may expand to several feet and radiate bright hues of gold or white. But if the same person is feeling threatened physically or emotionally, the entire aura may collapse to a much denser pattern within only a few inches of the body.

The Energy Field

Or

How We Contaminate Ourselves

I met this lady, Doris Crumpton; she was doing energy work, "The Emotion Code." The purpose of this code is to identify trapped emotions that are connected to our problem and then release them. It is a simple, yet very effective method. She has been certified for over a year and has been so inspired because she has seen it change people's lives, even with just one session. She has been doing other energy work for twenty years.

I had an idea of what she was doing, but not real clear. Because I am an explorer I thought I would try what she had to offer. This occurred within the last nine months. There are many people out there who have discovered healthy pathways through alternative means. Many people are very ill at ease, unhealthy and not in a good place, we seek out a physician and then we get a drug. Are we better? Probably not, maybe even worse. The alternative approach doesn't have the stamp of approval of the FDA or the powerful medical establishments. My contention is the FDA or the powerful medical establishments can't keep up with the flood of information that is coming to us today. But I believe doors are beginning to crack open. I believe our intuitive process, that is what feels right for us has to become the driver. Are you feeling the driver as you read this? As I write this I am smiling. Does it have a ring of truth for you? Maybe not, I hope it does.

A side note, about five months ago I had a knee problem. The pain was meddling so in my life I couldn't find a place of comfort. It contributed mightily to some of my sleepless nights. I found myself sleeping around, that was in every bed and in every room but the kitchen trying to find comfort. I was bed hopping. I first went to a chiropractor with no real improvement. I was willing to try acupuncture. I had it two times within a two week period. Well, thank goodness it worked. It was almost immediate. It has taken until now for this knee to feel like it's really okay, normal. But I haven't had that terrible pain. It is my understanding the acupuncture interferes with the neural pathway of the pain. The meridian lines in the body. I really don't totally understand how it works. Acupuncture is energy medicine. And it really works. If we imagine our livelihood to be threatened we lash out at whatever it is that we might think is threatening it. The medical establishment feels threatened by the alternative health practices. It might be an elitist attitude. I personally think it's a huge economic issue driven by lack. The fear that there isn't enough for everyone, physicians are some of the highest paid professionals on earth and as of late perhaps they have a fear of not having enough because their foundation is shaking. We are experiencing so many economic changes. The universe is abundant and has room for many modalities of healing. Now this doesn't mean that all of the people in the alternative medical world are effective or ethical nor does it mean the same is true for the medical profession. Once again, does it feel right? Does the treatment work? We set an intention, I want to feel better. We must ask and then *trust* we are being led by spirit on our journey to heal. I realized the result of the stated intention, in this instance it was acupuncture and that removed the pain for me.

Another question; how do we know what is worthy of recognition and what isn't? If it has a ring of truth for me then that is a sign that my inner knowing is confirming that I need to pay attention. So, back to Doris. She said she did energy clearing. She did her process with me over the phone. Under the guise of quantum physics this is possible. At first I thought oh is this going to be mumbo-jumbo or airy fairy as I used to say.

I will digress again. Once again I mention how we get information from our environment in the ways we are so familiar, that is our five senses. Otherwise we think anything is airy fairy or mumbo-jumbo. Well, what about this sixth sense? I have read some things and I believe intuition is associated with our pineal gland and our sixth chakra (energy centers in our bodies). I contend we are accessing information with our sixth sense even if we aren't aware and can't distinguish it. Consider we have these energy fields radiating from us as mentioned in the before information I pulled from the internet. Understand just because it's on the internet doesn't make it true. But what was I experiencing from my ex-husband when he was no longer present in this realm? My science background says explore and prove. Sometimes we keep hearing about a subject because we are so focused that we are drawing that information to us. That would be the law of attraction at work. I understand we are researching these energy fields. The Heart Math Institute has been investigating for over twenty years. I think their focus is the energy associated with the heart. That is a very interesting topic. I have heard the heart is a more powerful organ than the brain. The electromagnetic field of the heart is much larger than that of the brain; it has been measured to extend at least 8 feet from the body.

Anyway, can you tell I get side tracked, over the phone she went through a process, it was intuitive. Let me add here that there are muscle strength processes that provide information from the person's subconscious allowing negative energy to be transformed. I don't quite understand this but I trust it. Now the question is clearing what? Negative experiences we are holding onto or we picked up from someone else or maybe even from the previous generation. Negative experiences we aren't even aware of. Also remember everything is energy and energy transferring is occurring all the time. So we are back to our sixth sense. Once again, *"Everything is energy."* She asked me a series of questions the main one that I remember was about me experiencing a certain emotional quality in reference to my father. It had to do with abandonment and she said it was associated with my father. I said yes to that and didn't realize until I was off the phone how really true it was. Well, my father's father left them when my dad was six years old. The last time he saw him he was tagging along behind him. He flipped him a nickel and they never saw him again. He left my grandmother with four boys and they were put out of the house. She was abandoned with a family to care for alone. For me this had a definite ring of truth.

Now, Doris said that energy can be transferred to children. At the time I was thinking now how can this be. Remembering: energy is transferred and when two people come together their energy bodies entangle. Strong emotional patterns negative or positive enhance the quantity and quality of the quantum entanglement. My dad came into the relationship with my mother and he was carrying this abandonment issue as well as other issues. Their offspring, me, would have received some energy patterns from them. Just by being associated with them some of the energy transfers to me. When this energy healer, as I call her, told me this I was amazed and thought how this has a ring of truth for me. His father was never a topic for discussion. The most I heard him say was a statement or two and when spoken there was this sting of strong resentment; he said how he was so angry with his father for doing this to him. His emotional overtones were the telling tale. This was a negative experience my father held for a lifetime and maybe longer. I definitely felt better and clearer after experiencing "The Emotion Code" with Doris. I dare say the experience my father had definitely affected his relationship with us as he was always there for us.

It is my opinion at this stage of my life considering my biology background, my counseling background, my exploring nature, and my life experiences that there is far more to "it" than we see with our five senses. "It" meaning all that is, God to infinity. And there is so much more than we even begin to understand with our current understanding of how things work. We must remain open and unlock our boxes of prearranged thought and step out of the box as they say. I even feel that we are on an accelerated path of human development and the intention is that we are to grow and expand our awareness as a species. Our experiences are the journey we make when we grow and become more in tune with spirit. We evolve to a better place moment by moment. Step by step. I have my own ideas and I am sharing them with you in this book. I am just thinking out loud. It is my intention that you will find something helpful from these pages. And that you enjoy.

I imagine our energy body being like the old postal boxes, little cubicles, and we store away these emotional energy patterns. My memories are mostly memories of emotion. I recall how I felt but don't necessarily recall words. The emotions then become part of our total package and we function within our environment holding this negative or positive energy. It's in our box. When we are harboring resentment from a particular incident it's stored in our energy body and it can interfere with our health, especially if there is strong intense emotion with this resentment. How much power are we giving to the incident that we are holding onto? Is it a passing emotional thought? Have we dwelled upon it? Have we given our lives to it? I have always heard my mother say when you hate someone it only hurts you. Well I kept trying to figure out how that could be. It's a spiritual concept. Because we are storing this nasty little pesky piece of energy, whatever it might be, it then becomes part of us. We are contaminating ourselves with this stuff we harbor against another. It in turn can make us ill. We are doing it to ourselves. All energy vibrates, and at different rates. We are akin to tuning forks. We are vibrating so we react and attract according to our vibrating energy field. You know, those vibes. Oh, those hidden agendas. We can't see them with our five senses but they control our behavior. We can feel them. Once we have a clearing or release the pocket of yuck emotion energy we begin to vibrate at a higher frequency. The higher frequencies are the places that make us feel the best and the healthiest. The places we call heaven. *Places* is a poor choice of word but how do you define it, consciousness, maybe. We are defining our world with our emotions; they are powerful and have huge impacts on the quality of our lives.

Now if I am 68 and just beginning to understand this concept of clearing, oh my, that's 68 years of programing plus whatever came to me from past generations or possibly the consciousness from another life. Just sayin.

Good Vibes Bad Vibes

Einstein tells us we are energy. Everything is energy. Gosh, I haven't already told you this, ha, I just had to say it again. I guess it's my astonishment at the realization of this concept so I have to keep telling myself and you. Why do we "feel" uncomfortable with some people and not others?

Recently, I heard a talk by Dr. Bruce Lipton who wrote "The Biology of Belief." He was talking about good vibes and bad vibes. We all have talked about these and use these same words often. Now the scientist in me says "hey, what's going on here?" just as Dr. Lipton. Well he gave me an explanation that was just so cool. I thought this rings true for me so I am passing this along here.

We receive information from our environment through our senses. With our eyes we see energetic waves and our brain turns the signals into pictures. When we receive sound waves, we have picked up the messages from the patterns in the air molecules. The patterns were caused by something disturbing the air molecules. The air molecule disturbances are then perceived as sound by our brains. Did I hear that bell? All of those patterned air molecules received by my ear allowed the sound to be heard by my brain as that bell. I think this is very unique, an awesome human adaptation allowing us to interact with our environment. What a creation and its basis is the ability to receive information from the energy in our environment. We have these special sensors that detect energy and our brains convert it into information. We experience the environment with our five senses. And our sixth sense also, what about that mysterious sixth sense?

I think energetic vibrations are better understood when we explore the quantum atom. The quantum atom is a little different from the atoms most of us learned about in school that is the diagram of a nucleus containing all the little illustrated balls named protons and neutrons and tiny electron specks dashing around the outer edges of the atom. The quantum atom really has no structure but is a *vibrating* nano tornado. Nano is a prefix meaning billionth or 0.000,000,001. To help understand the size of a nano: If you took a meter and divided it into one thousand equal pieces, one piece would be a millimeter. If you took a meter and divided it into one billion equal pieces, one piece would be a nanometer. I would say that's pretty small. All matter is composed of atoms. So everything is vibrating and when it vibrates it is shaking things up disturbing the area it's found in, making waves. A wave is a disturbance (an oscillation) that travels through space and time, accompanied by the transfer of energy. Energy can't be destroyed only transferred or transformed.

We are composed of billions of atoms all with their small nano tornadic spins. We are disturbing the areas around us with this vibration. Obviously that spin is disturbing something, the air? Perhaps that's what an aura is? Are all those atoms in motion making the energy field around the body? I have heard there is an ooze of electrons around us, just passing along information. This just so fascinates me. Life, its composition is pretty amazing. We are learning so many new concepts. Who is we I think it is me learning many new concepts.

If I drop a pebble into a pond I see the vibrating wave patterns spreading outward in rings. This is a wave pattern. If I drop two pebbles they will both make circles radiating outward. At some point they will touch and when they do the waves interact. When they come together this is called interference. It can be destructive interference when the waves are banging into each other or it can be constructive when the waves are meshing together. Okay, here you have two people and they both are vibrating on some level. Uh, oh, the waves are banging into each other, clashing. There go the "bad vibes." Okay, now we have two people coming together and their vibrations are constructive, I think you get the meaning. There go the "good vibes." Is this compatibility?

I think when our vibrations merge and there are emotional connections there is energy entanglement. Strong emotions love or hate, plus many experiences between two people over periods of time cause entanglements. These are the strong connections we feel between us and another. They are difficult to break and will/can cause us much emotional pain. We feel the result of the entanglement breaking as emotional pain and we say we are stressed. Stress is very personal. It changes our body chemistry and is the cause of up to 95% of our dis-eases.

If we are experiencing discordant energy or breaks in energy with someone we explain it with words that reflect our currently understood concepts. Most of us are totally unaware of who we are. When we know that we are part of the ALL that is, God. We are more able to handle the discordant energy. The "bad" vibes. We discover the importance of our words, our self-talk, our thoughts and our emotions in terms of vibrations. Our relationship to the world and the universe takes on a new light. How we think, the words we choose to speak about ourselves and our world is directly related to our emotional pain. We are always vibrating; the quality of the vibration is a result of all of our experiences, our thoughts and the words we use. You know that stuff we feel in our gut. We need to be aware so that we can make better choices about the words we use, how we use them, and what we are choosing to have in our lives. We have the power to change, we must first be aware. Those *words* are powerful tools for creating an abundant, healthy life. We have to go within to find the kingdom of heaven. I believe that is what we are told and heaven from my perspective is joy, peace and happiness. The words we choose to use define our joy, peace and happiness. The "good" vibes. Our emotional health determines our vibration frequency.

We will have instant recognition with another as if we have known them for a very long time. It is like we are one with them, our vibrations match. The energy waves are amplified they are constructive when we meet others with the same vibrational energy pattern as ourselves. It is my understanding the highest vibrational energy pattern is joy.

A Little Physics of Spirituality

Or

Inertia Busters

An object at rest will remain at rest unless acted on by an unbalanced force. An object in motion continues in motion with the same speed and in the same direction unless acted upon by an unbalanced force. This law is often called "the law of inertia," Newton's first law.

I have what I have called and will call *inertia busters*. These are circumstances, people or places that divert me in another direction. Life can be coasting along then all of a sudden it's time to change which I doubt I would actually do without a bump. I don't like change and even if circumstances are miserably familiar and I am somewhat comfortable with them I am going to stay put. But, it may just be in my best interest to change. I doubt I would change without an *inertia buster*. *Inertia busters* become the change agents that propel me onto another path. Our soul knows it's time to move and *inertia busters* bump us. I would have uncomfortable feelings; ones that really spoke to me and literally forced me to change direction. It doesn't always play out so easily there can be fierce personal struggles involved. Because these days I am more aware I am trying to be the "observer" hoping to see the need for change and do it easier. Sometimes the circumstances in my life would be like a huge storm with menacing clouds, lightening and strong winds or something like a mountain in my path. Other times it's something I don't like; it's an uncomfortable feeling (an emotion) that urges me to change the thought or the plan or just make a small change in direction. I am learning that a small change in the way I think changes the circumstances. Those pesky thoughts and the words I use to describe what I am experiencing set the tone for the experience. It helps to understand who I am. I am creating as I move through the storm. It is me, I am responsible. It's not anything "out there." Those words are mine. I am just responding to what has come into my environment. It's my storm and just managing enough time to endure it will help it pass. The familiar idea, feel the feelings and pass through them is something I'm still working on. The concept hasn't jelled with me. I can know something and then have an experience and then I own it. Other times I must have the experience again and again in order to own it. I walk down a street, there is a huge hole, I fall in and with much struggle and aid I am able to get out. I walk down the street, there is that hole I fall in but manage to cling to the side and crawl up and out. I walk down the street my foot begins to slip I catch it and pull back. I walk down the street and I walk around the hole. I walk down another street.

I had (past tense) a man in my life; I called him my *inertia buster*. Because of him I was propelled into making some major changes in the way I think, choosing the words I use to see my world and arriving at a healthier place mentally. Whew, that was some emotional storm. That was some journey. But I am healthier and in a better place. I even changed my outward circumstances and made some location moves because I was experiencing Newton's law "the law of inertia." I was propelled to change direction. I was going from point A to point B, the journey, and the change began by an inertia buster that jarred me in another direction because it certainly totally changed my circumstances. This was a time in this life that I so totally felt this thing we call love, I was so in love and it wasn't reciprocal, I believe it's called unrequited love. These circumstances put me in a very new place experiencing many new things. But the journey was very difficult. This has been within the last several years and it has taken me a while to recover. The storm of fear: of loss, of not being worthy of love, of not being acceptable, of rejection. The self-worth battle definitely made me look within. And of course that is where all the negative self-talk is that is creating my world of storm. The storm of emotions was definitely felt with my whole being. The intensity of pain was a measure of how strongly I was holding to those negative ideas about myself. I experienced the inertia buster, the unrequited love, and the experience allowed me to see how I was thinking about me. I was able to change my thinking to a more positive view of me. A change agent is a good thing. I am on my path to empowerment and I have stepping stones. Life really is a spiritual journey.

Newton's first Law, we sit on our buns until something comes along and bounces us onto another path. It was time to change; we set the idea in motion and then put the blame out there. Like the loss of a job. The underlying intention probably was the job just wasn't working for you anymore. You were crabbing and complaining about the messy job. Along comes the inertia buster, the change occurs, you lose the job. You're blaming everything out there for the change. Those sorry so and so's really messed me up. The real story, you were setting the intention with all the crabbing and complaining, I'm done and you were. The change agent, the inertia buster was the loss of the job; it turned out to be a good thing. It put you on another path and you discovered you were in a happier place. This scenario could apply to many things in our lives especially those things we are complaining about, remember the old adage be mindful of what you wish for, you just might get it. There is much truth in that statement. Be observant of your words, what are you wishing for? If only we could experience the good part quickly. I think we can if we own the change and don't project it all "out there."

A Part of The Universe

One of the points I am trying to make is for so much of my life I considered or thought of myself as not being a part of the universe as if somehow I removed myself from it. I was totally unaware that I couldn't subtract myself from the workings of the world of physics. Then I had this "ah" moment. Well, my goodness I am actually a part of this universe and subject to the laws of physics and chemistry. So I tried to think of things and circumstances that had dramatically impacted my life in terms of physics and chemistry. I coined the term inertia busters. I thought it fit well with Newton's first law. That is we pretty much stay on a road or path until something or someone comes along and jolts us in another direction.

When we look at our world and some of the unexplained events that we deny or just don't understand we might try looking toward science for answers. The sciences, physics, chemistry and biology can provide important clues about how life works. We are living in an information explosion there is so much new information it is rather mind bending. Because of my science background and the fact that I am an explorer, one of my passions is discovery. I have been through several shake-ups with my mental pictures of understanding how things work. I am disturbed when I can't place new ideas or experiences within my frame of reference. I like being able to give myself a satisfactory answer using the new information. Now understand this may not be the way they really work or the way they work for you but this is the way I have decided they work. I am using my science background and my life experiences to try and understand this merger between science and spirituality. My answer for this is: understanding energy helps explain spirituality. I think metaphysical and spirit may just have a kinship of sorts. How does spirit speak?

What is this oft referenced sixth sense? What in this world is going on there? Perhaps science and spirituality which to me are one in the same can provide some answers.

The Bible is filled many strange unexplained occurrences. I think the things that happened two thousand years ago can happen today. Our technology has been added to the scene making us think it can't be so.

For me one of the major problems with us humans is that there are seven billion of us and we all think we have the correct answer. And "I" am the one with the correct answer. I can see this as a creator of much argument and strife. *We are* creators of this messy violent stuff here on planet earth. There are seven billion correct answers. We all are seeing through the veil of the sum total of our own personal experiences. Whew, that's a lot of experiences! And we all think we are correct, especially when the ego is involved. Since we are all energy and we are all manufactured of the same stuff and we are all part of the universe and we are all governed by the laws of mathematics, physics and chemistry, I do believe I sense some sameness here. We are all one. So how do we get this separateness going on? Perhaps it's an illusion on the large scale which is the scale we are so accustomed to experiencing with our five senses. On the macro (large) level we definitely feel this separation because you're standing over there and I am over here we are definitely viewed as separate. But, perhaps this is not so on a micro level and the quantum-ness of it all, this is where we are one and the same. We are all energy and I suspect that the energy mingles. We are all pieces parts of the whole big thing, God, the Creator, the ALL that is, whatever you wish to call it. It's your choice. It's all the same God.

Just maybe this continual searching we all seem to be doing to find a connection between us and another is a result of this illusion of separation. The one we experience with our five senses. Another altogether different connectedness can be felt at a micro level utilizing our sixth sense, the one we associate with the sixth chakra. One of our body's energy centers. There is also the connectedness felt with our heart. That is also a chakra, the love connection, we actually feel this. We experience the essence of another. We are connected and we connect at many different levels.

I think that the ultimate connection is our personal perceived connection with God, cosmic intelligence, or the universal mind. God is totally personal. But, what is this? How does it work? How do we make this connection? Is it part of listening with our intuition and/or something felt? Just askin. One thing I am sure of its felt within.

Another Little Physics Law

For every action there is an equal and opposite reaction, this is Newton's third law. Man has had an understanding and the experience of this law for thousands of years. The Book of Ecclesiastes advises us to cast our bread upon the water for "At long-last, you will find it again." The great masters of spirituality have been telling us how this law works. In other words what goes out comes back. As we sow so shall we reap. In the metaphysical community it's called the law of reciprocity. In Eastern religions it's the law of karma.

Obviously we as a human species have in some manner known of this principle for a very long time. What we give out becomes energetic and can reach far beyond what we might expect. We may never realize how it has affected the world. What is given is not necessarily monetary but can be a smile, a pat on the back or a good word directed at someone. But, on the backside what we put out there might be tinged and not intended for the highest good of all, I think you get my drift. In any instance it is returned. This law operates as do all laws even if we deny them or we are totally unaware of the principle. It doesn't just apply to one word I say or one hand shake but actually everything I do goes "out there" to return to me at some later date.

My most compelling experience of this law, one that stands out and I can remember is the time I was riding with a friend. I had become so angered with someone, ah, can you guess, a man. Just jokingly I told her okay I'll carry the baseball bat and you drive the getaway car. And with very strong emotion I mentally could see that bat in my hand and I said with strong emotion "I would swing that bat and wham!" I was even using my arm to enact a small but power surged swing with emotion. Just about that time "this large thing" hit my windshield where I would have swung the bat. Yes, I had a huge three point ding. I said, oh, my gosh, look at that, and my friend said God is punishing you. My take on the matter I am responsible for what I put out there I created the circumstance, I sent out a strong burst of anger and it came back, rather quickly I might add and this was a huge lesson on a small scale. The windshield was repairable. I was/am definitely more mindful of what I am sending out there, or at least trying to be aware. I think I understand the law and how it works.

The laws don't just work sometimes they are laws they are always working.

I prefer love, joy and abundance in my life so I am working on being love, experiencing joy and abundance. I would like those life expressions to be returned to me. I might add I need to practice, practice, practice. How this law works I have no idea perhaps a trained physicist can explain it but I see it akin to Newton's third law. Maybe sowing and reaping, and the law of attraction are one in the same. That is what I am thinking.

Those Pesky Words

We are the sum total of all our thoughts, beliefs and the chemical reactions occurring within us. There is far more to us than we even begin to understand. It is our core beliefs, our thoughts and our body chemistry that make us healthy or unhealthy. Our molecules are constantly arranging and rearranging and always vibrating.

Let's talk "I am," "I am" is a statement referring to me and how I feel about me. "I am" can be neutral, worthy or unworthy. For example "I suck at health" or "I am a lousy parent." In both cases my core belief says: unworthy, I can't handle my health or parenting. Does that feel good? No! I have many core beliefs about many things. All the things I have learned all my life would be my core beliefs. They are stored in my subconscious and they drive my behavior. When I am doing consciousness work, observing and listening in terms of "I am" then I am assuming responsibility for me. It's me not you that is responsible for my behavior. If I am aware and listening then I can change the idea to "I am healthy" or "I am very worthy of parenting." Thus I have made a positive "I am" statement. It is a healthier statement that influences my core belief about me and that in turn influences my body chemistry. Does it feel good? Better, I hope and when I really "believe it," it has power.

Now let's think in terms of "you are." I am talking about the blame game. Such as I might say "you are so not right" especially connected with strong emotional overtones can be a very stinging statement directed at you. "You go to hell" or any of the other "you are" comments that are blaming or condemning. Blaming is a destructive energy pattern, bad vibes as we call them directed at another. Those feeling of hitting a brick wall when someone sends a zinger. The words are harsh and can really sting. The energy springing forth from the person is negative energy and the entire body can experience an intense reaction to the caustic words immediately. My entire body reacts to zingers; it's like a body flash. Often the words keep repeating over and over thus creating the feeling pattern over and over again. It's experiencing the entire event in a closed loop over and over in our mind. Do I want to own what comes to me from someone else, especially if it's their junk? No! Do I understand those harsh blaming words don't belong to me but to the person expressing them? I am still working on not accepting other people's zingers. *I understand this concept but I am still feeling zingers so I must take a look at my issues, I am the one responsible for my pain.* We are like balls bouncing off of each other to clear our negative stuff and find a better feeling place. Personally I am a work in progress. I am still reacting. "I am" assumes responsibility for me "you are" is the opposite. It's not my job to tell you what or who you are. I can tell you who "I am."

Whatever we are expressing is a result of what is going on within us always, one hundred percent of the time. Relationships are about clearing, clearing, clearing. It's like peeling away the scales of an onion removing one layer at a time. We are always evolving and experiencing higher and higher vibrational patterns with each layer removed. When we become enlightened we have found that place of joy. Our negative vibrational patterns have been transformed. We are like the Nobel Gases, complete and non-reactive. Ha, I don't think I'm a Nobel Gas yet.

Nobel Gases are a group of elements found on the periodic table. They have all their electron shells complete, filled with eight electrons. Eight is the magic number. All atoms combine with other atoms so they can have eight electrons in their outer most shell. Now salt is made from sodium and chlorine. Sodium has 1 electron in its outer most shell and chlorine has 7 electrons in its outer most shell.

If sodium has 8 within and 1 outer and chlorine has 7 outer and they remain isolated and alone they are both very reactive. They are very willing to give up an electron or grab one, wham! They come together in a flashy exchange releasing energy. Remember the magic number eight; they are soooo needy of each other to complete the magic number eight. Once together they both have eight electrons in their outer shell creating the more stable less reactive compound, salt. This is the way I used to explain basic chemistry concepts to my students and then I heard Dr. Bruce Lipton explain it the same way but then he said it was like codependence. We were all amazed when he said this. It was like a collective AH! One atom really needs the other to be complete. But, Nobel Gases can stand alone they already have the magic number of 8 electrons. Now when two Nobel Gasses get together there is no reacting they are already complete and that's like two enlightened people. It is pure pleasure; they can both coexist interdependently, no codependent. Dr. Bruce Lipton is a most amazing speaker. He explains spirituality in science terms. I like that. I consider him to be an enlightened human being; he might just be like a Nobel Gas.

Relationships are for understanding oneself. They're for clearing and reaching finer energy patterns. Love is a much higher vibration frequency than hate. Feel those emotions. Feel them with your heart center. What are the vibrational patterns of love and hate? I haven't seen them. But I have felt them. I bet they have been measured and I would imagine they have very different signatures.

When we speak in terms of "I am" we are working on ourselves. When we speak in terms of "you are" we are putting the blame outside of ourselves. We make ourselves the victim. Ultimately everything is within us. What often happens when we are codependent we are still putting it out there. "I am" is on the path to empowerment. "You are" is on the path to pain. Just sayin, stripping away the layers and evolving.

Emotions

Or

Those Pesky Things We Don't Know How to Handle

Emotions are defined as strong feelings about someone or something, a heightened feeling. Another definition linked with this one is agitation caused by a strong feeling.

Well, now that tells me bunches about emotions. How about:

Emotions are something we feel that causes us to change direction and pushes us toward new paths.

Emotions can speak so loudly they can become like a raging storm that can be classified as anxiety/panic.

Emotions are those "things" we feel moving through our entire body. The instant chemical and electrical messages the brain and mind sends to the body.

Our bodies tingle; feel the wave? Something, a stirring happening within, is this emotion? Just recently someone was calling my attention to the fact that I had taken a little extra time, more than they thought necessary. There was no time limit. I instantly felt the sharp pang of criticism. It was my feeling I owned it. I was very aware of the wave of feeling that rushed through my body, I lost my focus, my power of concentration and I blew the task at hand. I have set an *intention* at this point in my life to be the observer of me. My emotions were speaking to me and they were strong enough that I lost my focus and was not performing as I could have. I didn't like this experience at all. I didn't like feeling this way or allowing someone else to affect me in such a manner. I had a full blown negative emotional reaction and in this instance I could feel its power. Have you experienced this too? I am aware of learning very early that I wasn't supposed to feel negative emotions. But, I did, they were always there just like the elephant hiding in the living room under the rug that no one could see. Ha! They affected my behavior just like they do today. Emotions push me to find a better feel good place in life.

How about those quirky things we experience when someone says something nasty and we shoot back a response. Or they say something very nice and we feel all warm inside. I much prefer feeling the warm fuzzies as opposed to the harsh pricklies. The above incident was giving me pricklies.

All of the above are related to emotions. If I Google emotion tons of information surfaces.

Personally for me I remember emotions or feelings connected to events in my life. I don't necessarily remember the words but I can tell you how I felt at the time. Are emotions stored in our bodies? Yes, I think so otherwise why would I remember them. And today there are modalities we can use to remove them.

So emotions are connected to my words and the result is feeling. What came first the chicken or the egg? Is it words create feelings or we have feelings and then try to describe them? How do we describe, put into words that "thing" we are experiencing within the very core of our being, our heart center and our gut. How do we describe that uncomfortable wave of emotion? That's part of the mystery. It's difficult to define, words are inadequate to describe, so we tell the story in hopes the emotional content will be conveyed. Some people are very good at this; some motion pictures are excellent at relaying emotional content causing an upheaval within us by just observing the movie. When I leave some movies I am saying, whew! That totally wore me out. I don't like that and don't want to experience any more movies of that nature. Emotions direct my behavior. The mystery of it all, it gives my mind something to do.

I always felt that emotions had an adaptive advantage for us as a species otherwise we wouldn't be experiencing them. Mayhap they give us the qualifiers we need to explain and define our life experiences, our lives that are composed of opposites, both sides of the coin, the good and the bad. Emotions help us evolve and grow. The bad, the uncomfortable helps us convert to gold, that is the alchemy of spirituality. The negative helps us to find the good it's a transformation.

I think it's safe to say our words are of the utmost importance. Words define our world and our experiences. We feel reactions to the words or the event. Our feelings are measurements of how we are functioning in a given situation. They are a measure of our peacefulness.

There are many words we use to describe emotional states such as sadness, joy, love, happiness, fear, anger and the list goes on. There are many, many experiences one can have associated with these feeling states. Recognizing them can be a challenge.

I like simplistic answers because too much information tends to confuse me. I can see too much in my arena of life and I shut down. So, I propose there is love and fear. These two, love and fear bring us together or spread us apart. All of the other words we use to describe emotion are spin-offs from these two basic emotions. This is my opinion. I am sure you have your opinion. But I like to try to follow the KISS principle that was introduced to me early in my life when I first started teaching school and thought I could change the world. Ha! Well, I was told *keep it simple* and the other "s" is *stupid*. At the time I was so overwhelmed with all the information coming my way. I just kind of ignored the insult of being called stupid. I remember this from long ago and today I am not going to own what someone thinks or says about me. Whatever they say, the judgments they make belongs to them. How I respond belongs to me. For me this is a basic spiritual principle. And I am reminded continuously of this especially when I am having my "button's" pushed. My emotional responses are not always loving. No kidding, maybe the Dali Lama has this all under his belt. But I am a work in progress just like peeling an onion. We get one layer off and guess what there are layers and more layers.

The importance of emotions is they give me clues to understanding where I am in space and time. I become aware of what I need to work on and how I can evolve to a place that is more loving and less stress-filled. The emotions of my life: wow, of course as in everyone's life, we are reacting to the words and circumstances in our world. My life has had many challenging circumstances following that yellow brick road. I'm off the see the wizard did you hear my heels click? I am searching for answers as I move through the process of exploring, understanding and making sense of my life. It all just is! I am *hoping* the rest of my life is much more peace filled than the first part. I'm going to change hoping to: my life is going to be more peace filled. Hoping is "it might be." My intention is my life is *going* to be more peace filled. Uh, oh, going to be "is in the future." How is this: my life is more peace filled right here and now. Yes, that's it! It's been an interesting, but very challenging time. And when my buttons are pushed I hope to resolve my own inner conflict and not become a turtle. How do I do that? Not sure, perhaps, I ask to be shown, acknowledge it, accept the feeling and move past it.

Once again my old standby we are energy, just vibrating at a certain frequency that allows us to experience this earth plain. I am a product of all the atoms found here on this planet. Atoms are tiny little vibrating tornadoes that arrange and rearrange themselves to be me so I can experience this reality. My mom ate the cabbage, beets, turnips and beef and wow, the atoms were rearranged to become me. Today I eat the celery, beans and greens and it becomes me and fuels me. Pretty cool! Yes!

I have read information that says emotions are tiny little packets of energy. If I can remember emotions they must be stored somewhere.

Not only do we store all the emotions we have experienced in this life time but even during our nine months of development. We carry packets of energy from our parents into this world, the energy is transferred from them to us and then it becomes ours. Little bundles of negative energy, negative emotion energy, that come through them into us as we are conceived from that egg and the sperm. Remember energy transfers. There is more to us than we really understand at this point in time. I am asking what was the emotional content of the mother and father? What emotions were they experiencing independently and together has a couple in their relationship? What was the quality of their quantum entanglement? What were they passing on to us? What did they have passed to them from their parents? And what did we experience during those nine months of development? What kinds of stress was the mother under? What neuropeptides was she passing on to the developing fetus? What quantum entanglement occurred between the mother and father and the children? I'm just asking energy questions. I really don't think we are all as separated as we think.

I have always thought that emotions were contagious. Are we radiating? Someone walks in and the whole area changes. You talk to someone playing the "ain't it awful game," and in a very short period of time you're "ain't it awful." Someone is feeling so forlorn and you talk to them, yep, forlorn has become you. Energy transfers. What if we are also collecting emotions that aren't ours? This is a world of energy. Smiling, you think I like this concept of energy. It's amazing to me.

An afterthought; I was driving home one afternoon back in the early summer last year and I was ruminating over something and it was making me angry. My thoughts were focused on my feelings about how I had been "treated" by another. Someone cut me off. I was so outraged, I was totally hollering and I was in extreme anger. I thought I was literally going to explode and have a stroke right then and there. I could feel my body's reaction. It was a very scary moment. I don't think I want to do that again.

Trusting Intuition

I have always been interested in life, death, what's it all about? I have been on this incredible journey of discovery. It seems I am just settling into feeling comfortable with many of the experiences on my journey. I have tried to explain then somehow.

I was very interested in "death" as our present culture experienced it and the beliefs surrounding it. Back in the seventies I was very intent on finding out more about death. At the time I was reading Elizabeth Kubler Ross and getting her expert opinions on death and dying. I believe at the time my ex-father-in-law was going through his bout with cancer which ultimately allowed his transition. I just didn't understand anything about death. What was this thing called death? Somehow during that time I was introduced to NDE's that is near death experiences. At that time they were very hush hush. We just didn't want to discuss such foreign scary experiences in "polite" society. People might think we are crazy. Perhaps there are more experiences than just NDE's to tell us things maybe more than they seem.

My experience with my ex-husband being here trying to communicate with me after he had made his transition is a little out of the ordinary. I was rather selective who I shared this story with; people might think I am crazy. I have since read a book about others who have had this happen. A book by Dr. B. Stone called "Invisible Roots" says I have company. I think I was not so aware of my intuition at the time nor was I listening to it. So the universe's plan was to get my attention. Yes, it got my attention. I was and still am so curious about life everything about it and always asking questions and looking at it as an explorer would. As a child I read the "Book of Knowledge" encyclopedias. Bring out the geek squad. I don't wear a plastic pocket protector or have tons of pens in my pocket. They are in my purse. Ha! Just kidding. I do have about 4 pens in my purse. Gosh I was a teacher. I loved pens and pencils, they have a special magic, and they are the direct link to what is in my consciousness as I transfer those thoughts to paper. That in itself is marvelous. My hand is connected to my brain and you know the hip bone is connected to the . . . and so the old rhyme goes. It seems as if everything is connected on some level, it's all energy.

I have always wanted to know more. So what more was there than just my five senses could tell me? What else might there be other than the things that are so tangible like touch, feel, taste, smell and see. Today, I believe our sixth sense, that sense of knowing, is very vital and healthy and a knowledgeable way to understand more. Intuition has been virtually ignored by our society, even denied. Because of our beliefs we have thought it to be invalid and weird and not tangible so therefore it just didn't exist. There have been people with varying degrees of intuition that were willing to share this with us and they were on the outer fringes of society, the psychics.

I have often wondered what this sixth sense stuff is. How do I recognize the "voice?" I have been more aware of my intuition as of late obviously it has been with me always but my ability to recognize its importance or its value was nonexistent. Perhaps we have too many distracters, too much information coming in to be able to distinguish the inner voice. If I am living within the constraints of society's beliefs, I would think intuition just was not so. How do I distinguish it from the other rumblings in my brain? And I suspect I have followed it unaware and unknowing just thinking it is me. But in the last several years as I have progressed on my life journey with spirit listening has become more important for me. I am just beginning to be able to distinguish this inner voice. Writing this book has been an experience that has allowed me to learn to listen better. I now have an inkling of what it sounds like and *trusting* that what I am listening to is going to be beneficial. If I want to listen with my spiritual self then I need to learn how to listen with my sixth sense. How else would I know if spirit is talking to me? It might just be through anything in this world, even electronics. If it worked for the aboriginal man then it should be working for us. This is just the rumblings of my brain as I explore intuition. If I ask a question and expect an answer, what do I do to listen for the answer? What do I expect? We are either totally of the universe or it's all a crap shoot. We can't be half and half. If we are of the universe then we are immersed in it and the laws are always working. We must work within those laws. Spirituality is the law. Such as what we send out returns to us not just some of the time but all the time. It's not just a little karma here and a little karma there it's always working.

My traditional earth educational background was science based, a biology teacher by university training. The first concept I taught my students was biology is the study of life. Bio= life and ology = the study of. My second degree was counseling because at the time I thought it was one of the ways to have a better understanding of people especially the students I was teaching. And it was paid for by the state because they saw a need for placing counselors in all schools. They needed a large number of counselors so they helped fund our education. Yes! It was a great benefit for the state and for me. Thank you. So I saw an opportunity: an advanced degree, an advanced salary, a more financially secure retirement and an opportunity to help others. During the early nineties when I was working on my counseling degree I didn't learn anything about death or listening to one's intuition. Counseling is about life issues. Intuition wasn't recognized as a valid way to gather information from ones environment. I certainly don't even begin to understand it all. But my understanding is much better than any other time in my life. It's listening to the quiet voice within and being still long enough to actually listen. And *trusting*, trusting that the truth is there for my benefit. We are talking type A personality here. Sitting still isn't easy and just maybe I tagged myself as type A but I'm not really an A. My life took on too much and I had to run to keep up. That would take on the appearance of type A.

So, getting back to the NDE's I mentioned earlier. I go to a group that allows people who have had NDE's to have a place to vocalize their experiences. Mostly people aren't interested in hearing about other people's NDE experience because they consider then to be "off the wall," they frighten them as they aren't experiences that are easily tasted, smelled, touched or seen. They are so intangible. The unseen is so scary for our culture and our current understanding of life and its place in the universe. The people who had NDE's have had "life changing" experiences and they have difficulty finding someone who will listen and understand. We are there to listen and we get to expand our own awareness.

I consider my story a little different, a little far out there and life changing. Now I've had an ODE, other dimension experience. How would I have connected with my ex-husband after he had made his transition other than intuition or would it be a psychic connection? There was something happening through thought transference or energy transference, maybe it was both. Before I discovered my ex-husband was hanging out with me I was thinking everything emotional and mental was totally mine. I was really struggling and thought I was totally losing it. Perhaps that isn't always the case. Actually before he made his transition I jokingly said hey, when you get over there see if you can send me a message or something. Let me know if there really is something there. This may even be an explanation with lots of holes, but for right now it's working for me.

I must say before this incident my belief system was gradually changing but for some time I thought we are here, products of this earth and we are flip flopped around and then we die, period. I would say my belief system isn't even close to that this day.

For many years now when I misplaced something I would throw out the thought or speak out loud, okay, help me find it, lost object speak to me. And somehow I was/am led to it. It always shows. There is something energetic going on. I don't know I just know it works.

Not long ago I was going to drive over to Mississippi, I do like to gamble a little. I had this voice that said *don't go*. I should have listened. A guy ran a red light and I ran into him. The first wreck I ever had. He had no insurance. The good point: the policeman was sitting at the intersection and he observed the whole thing. Fortunately, my car was fixable. My driving has improved. I am more conscious of defensive driving these days.

I should have listened. Should have, could have make a path for regret. I think I would like to delete those terms should have and could have.

It is my opinion that the Native Americans and the indigenous peoples of the world were very in touch with the lands they inhabited on earth. They were very intuitive. They were listening to spirit with great respect. My story, I think says we can listen in our world too. Spirit is spirit regardless of the circumstances. Are we listening with respect to our earth?

Mindfulness

This is a conversation with a cousin of mine that I have just reconnected with on Facebook. I probably haven't seen him since he was a young boy age five or six and he was the cutest little guy he had the most gorgeous eye lashes. We all wanted his eye lashes. He just recently told me he didn't like them I guess he thought they were too feminine, he grew up in a very masculine family. We were chatting and talking about the victim role in our society. We had been sharing an article about the power one felt from being a victim. A victim can be defined as somebody who experiences misfortune and feels helpless to remedy it. And they can use this role to control others. Oh, woe is me. Oh, did you see what they did to me. Or there is the "ain't it awful" game. I used to play the "ain't it awful" game a lot while teaching school. I still play it when talking about the conditions of our world today, especially our government. I try not to become pulled into this mode of thought its nonproductive nothing is solved and it produces restlessness. This conversation is word for word, stream of consciousness as we chatted online.

Me: Yes indeedie we are victims we just decided not to choose the victim words once we are aware of what the words are. Then we can play another role. When we are choosing victim words we are playing with victim power. I like success words, and then we play the success role. Words, words, words . . . . the POWER of words.

My cousin: Well said cuzzzz! What is sad is that when you choose to gain power in this manner, as a victim, it will, in reality, be a self-destructive power. It may get you what you want for the moment but eventually this type of karma will come to a fruition you don't like.

Me: Thanks CUZZZZZZ Well are we talking: NOT much joy and happiness or bliss. I have been in the victim mindset I didn't like it. I have been in lots of mind sets playing many roles and most of them didn't give me much joy, happiness or bliss. So I am now trying to be mindful of what I am thinking(those pesky words) or saying and change the words, then I change the feelings then I change my world. Mindfulness. Living in the moment. Go mindfulness! My cheer for the day.

Can you tell we are cousins? We like it exaggerated. My cousin is younger than me so I really didn't have much of a connection with him as a child as I was the older one. I was fourteen when he was born. That gave me power. Ha! Ha! The ego really was working overtime then and still is. I knew everything. Ha! Ha! He was just a little kid getting into everything. I was an adult, yes, at fourteen. Oh mercy me at fourteen, I was so needy. Those hormones were talking to me and all the great love songs of the fifties, the emotionally charged words just spoke to all of us. We all wanted love, we still do. Oh my goodness. Where did this idea take *you* when you clicked your heels and walked the yellow brick road? Life lessons abound. It's been an interesting road . . . Mindfulness is being aware of what is in this moment, refining and moving forward.

How To Speak Swahili

Or

How to Recognize Psychic and Intuitive

Well, I have been to Africa on safari and was in the area where Swahili was spoken. Now I would need the foreign language program that promotes learning a language with ease. Perhaps I should try this program. I think we are all familiar with the advertisement: learn languages without effort just naturally like you were a small child again. I am monolingual and this language program would give me an opportunity to prove myself incorrect. I could learn another language. But I probably won't accept that challenge because I have accepted the challenge to learn to recognize my intuition. I now understand that psychic experiences are very real. And as I think back and review my life some things I thought were just nothing could be intuition rumblings as well as some psychic experiences.

One of my questions though out this life was what is this that can't be seen? What have I been experiencing? What is this thing we call intuition? How do I know if I am experiencing intuition? What does intuition mean? My science background said knock my socks off. Well, the few encounters I had with "psychics" were hit and miss on the information they provided me. I was a little familiar with the well know psychics that have been in the media. I was skeptical. But, Teresa Brown gave me a glimpse of what an intuitive medium can do. I think she has an amazing gift that gives her the ability to recognize the energies of people who are in another realm. I think I understand it's the energy of organisms the psychics can read. I think the difference between intuition and psychics: intuition is listening to God and psychic is reading some ones energy or thoughts. But Teresa identifies herself as an intuitive-medium. I think she has the best of both worlds.

So, investigating and exploring and sorting all the information I have discovered has provided me with more knowledge and understanding. All of the experiences I have encountered have definitely confirmed that there is another realm that I was totally unaware of. Our culture doesn't validate obtaining information from the sixth sense or reading other peoples energy. I don't begin to understand it all but everything is energy. I now must rearrange my old paradigm to include all of what I have experienced which includes recognizing intuition and being psychic. I must think of these in terms of energy.

And mostly I must trust myself that my evidence is real.

One of our most basic concepts of religion is prayer; we are talking to God that is usually through thought. And then we listen for answers. Is this not intuition? I suppose it's all in the semantics. Are psychics using intuition? For most of my life psychics have always seemed a little airy fairy but at the same time I was very interested. There is so much controversy surrounding their abilities. Now, I have to change my paradigm. My thinking has to go outside my original box to explain what I considered abnormalities in my world: people with way out there notions that are talking to people no longer here. Well, guess what, way out there notions are here especially after my experiences. Energy can be detected by our body as vibrations and probably more but I am just a beginner. This is pretty new for me. The shared experiences in these "Bits & Pieces" are how I got to this point in my thinking. This is a biologist's journey into spirit. The content of this book is an attempt to explain my understanding of how things work at this very moment. And a month from now I will have to adjust again. I feel the need to remain open-minded because so many things I thought not so seem to have some validity. Things seem to be happening at break neck speed. Well, not break neck, just great speed. No more broken necks. I have been there and done that. Ouch!

There is just so much more than I ever considered. The possibilities are infinite in this uni-verse, even multi-verse. Now the physicists are saying there are more universes. To get to the "more" one must be still and quiet and listen, smiling here, try that for a type A personality like me. Some people are so open to listening it's second nature to them. They say we all have the ability some of us have had it squelched or we just aren't aware that some of our thoughts aren't our own. Now if thoughts are energy we send them "out there" all the time then we are broadcasting just like the radio stations. If this isn't so, why pray? Energy is being sent out there all the time in the form of radio and TV. Of course radio stations and TV have amplifiers to boost their signals. I understand that a few of the first "Dr. Who" science fiction programs from the earlier days, late fifties to early sixties, have hit something out there and have bounced back and we are receiving them. In fact some of the ones they are receiving are lost programs. So now they can complete their library of "Dr. Who" episodes. Be mindful of what you ask for you just might receive it. I have heard that said many times, not just about radio shows. We may have amplifiers also, I am just not sure what they are, I suspect strong emotion is an amplifier along with focused thought. I am remembering the cloud dissipating experiences were done with focused thought.

I don't know much about intuition or how to be psychic. My science background says prove it. I have to say that we are beginning to have the technology to do just that. But the incidences in my life have provided me with the understanding that there is more, much more. If I can just step outside the box of how I think things are supposed to be. WOW! That's a huge "ah!" moment for me. I am having many "ah!" moments as of late. They seem to be tumbling in at a fast rate. It must be that out of the box thinking I have been doing. I'm just trying to be open-minded to possibilities. I am learning to determine and select and listen and guess what? *It's* not all mine. So what I have thought was all mine just isn't because of a newer understanding about energy coupled with my science background. We are energy it spills over and it transfers. Just possibly every thought I think is mine really isn't! Psychic, if I have this ability, would enable me to pick up on other's thoughts. I think I was doing this with my ex-husband. I have experienced this before with other people. Knowing something about them then it would be so and especially if I had an emotional connection with them.

I had my socks knocked off. One of the most astounding recognitions was the fact that my ex-husband was hanging around me after his transition as mentioned earlier. I was experiencing his emotions probably along with others. Where was all that anxiety coming from? I own some of it, but the intuitive-medium, Teresa said I was picking up on his stuff, experiencing it as if it was my own. But whatever it's gone and that is totally awesome. The anxiety/panic: I was reading energy, another's energy. I am learning how to understand and listen and participate with this new information that is unfolding for me. I am trying to learn to recognize my psychic abilities. As well as explore my unity with spirit, God energy, through intuition. God energy is everywhere. Are we like fish swimming around in the water looking for water? Where is the water I say to my favorite fish friend? And he says what water? I don't see any water. And a huge whale swims by and jumps out of the water. It has disturbed the whole area sending us tumbling. It's like being in the air, do you see any air? I don't! But I experience the evidence for it. We're in the God energy.

When I look at my whole life at least the one that started in 1943 it all makes sense, a learning process of empowerment. My current job is to be more aware, live in the moment, be mindful, and try to understand my purpose as it unfolds. I am to be part of the creative process for consciousness expansion and evolution on earth. When I am aware of my own negative energy and transform it I am helping the planet bit by bit. It helps clear the way for us all when we each do our part. All 7 billion of us are adding to the collective consciousness of humanity. We add to it in a positive way or a negative way. Our worldwide culture has so much negative *energy* such as hate, war, anger and greed. I think if the positive doesn't balance out the negative, Oh, I am just thinking what might happen. Are we out of balance? Nature is always seeking a steady state, homeostasis.

There is so much nasty energy, hate, fear and greed. Mercy, who wants to indulge in those emotions, we all have a choice. I have a choice and I would rather choose peace, love and gratitude. These are the "places" with which I wish to align. To do this I must be aware of my thinking and what I am creating moment by moment. What am I feeling? Feelings are tickets to a better place if we are listening we can discover what we need to change but first of all we must be honest with ourselves. Own the feelings, and then change the words. I am on my way to empowerment to co-create and bring heaven to earth. And so it is. Namaste means I bow to you as I recognize the Divine spark within you, spirit bowing to spirit. Namaste.

So Fortunate To Have Traveled

I have been so fortunate to have been able to travel to several places. I have done NSTA, National Science Teachers Association workshops. When I was teaching I loved to do this it was always so informative. At one conference I was watching a presentation from the San Diego Zoo. All those great animals they shared with us. Afterwards I was hanging around wasting time until the next presentation and a little penguin came strolling by. He was so close and so few people were left that I just had to explore. I was pretty close and was able to get an up close and personal "look see." There was a guy standing close to me in a suit with a red shiny tie. He leaned over his tie reacted to the gravity. Oops, there went the tie; the penguin swallowed it right up to the tie knot at his neck. It was so fast. There was the tie, the tie was gone. That was funny. He had to pull the tie back up out of the penguins gut. Ew, probably a bit fishy.

I got to experience London, England. Walking up the wallowed out worn steps into Westminster Abby was thrilling. I just wanted to stand there and experience the moment. The thrill of it all walking where it's safe to say millions have walked. I was exchanging air molecules with all the people that were there and had inhaled them before me. It was just so amazing I could just *feel* the history of it all. I loved this place called England. I know that one of my ancestors can be traced back through my mother's father; he came from Kent County around 1530. But just in the last three months my cell phone keeps showing me information about the Battle of Hastings;

I have no idea why this topic keeps popping up. I will get ready to send a text message and all of sudden this information about the battle appears on my screen. Well, guess what I just looked up the battle? The battle was on October 14, 1066. That's my birthday, of course not 1066. Smiling. I have heard that the places, the countries that draw our attention are places we have probably lived in the past that could be a past life. I have read that significant dates are clues as well. And I have heard that families reincarnate in groups, a good reason to do a genealogy study. This information comes psychologists and psychotherapist like Dr. Brian Weiss who have done hypnotic regression on thousands of individuals and have recognized patterns that occur within their research data. There is a suburb in London that is the same name as my maiden name; I bet there is a connection. Perhaps that line of my family can be traced back to this little town.

If spirit is having an earthly experience and spirit is helping to evolve life on this planet, then it would make sense that it comes in, life happens and then spirit leaves. Life can be pretty rough. I hear people say "I really wouldn't want to live through all those years again." I have said this too. The human bodies' design is such that it can only tolerate just so much then it has to go back to its origin. Dust to dust and ashes to ashes. And Spirit goes back into the ethers. Spirit needs to rest, resolve, and determine what was learned in this life. And just possibly set another intention and have another life time. Laws of the universe unknown to me are effecting what happens on the other side as well as this side.

I have been to Alaska, oh wow, the pristine environment, the vast stretches of nothing but nature. It was wonderful, a little chilly. There were so many eagles all in one place, such a brilliant sight to behold. There were moose wandering around everywhere. Mount McKinley just didn't want us to see the top; it was veiled in its own weather system. But just about a minute before we left the clouds parted and it shared its top with us. I envisioned our resort deck toppling over as we all rushed to the edge to see this spectacular view.

It's so large it makes its own weather system. The highest peak in North America it's the center of Denali National Park and Preserve and it's a most impressive sight.

I have been to Austria and Hawaii. They were adventures of a different climate and both unique in their expression. There were many lovely things to experience in each place. I was able to visit cousins and an aunt in each area. I was also fortunate to go on a Baltic cruise: a tour of the Scandinavian countries, St Petersburg, Russia and Estonia. How lovely it was, just beautiful, exploring and discovering these unique places.

Italy, oh the statue of David just took me by surprise as I walked in the room I was overwhelmed at the size, I gasped at the talent of Michelangelo. It's a masterpiece, a larger than life Renaissance sculpture created between 1501 and 1504, it's totally amazing. Michelangelo was a master. When we arrived at Assisi and looked down on the valley below it was all cloudy except for one shaft of light shining through a hole in the clouds, what an emotion filled moment. And the ruins at Pompeii were pretty amazing. Italy has beautiful doors I loved the doors and so much romantic history. I learned so much history. Italy was a bus tour it was very tiring but we covered so many of the most fascinating places.

Okay, for a biology teacher, the piece de resistance was Africa. The natural environment! The noted absence of man! Here are treasures of life that just might not make it another hundred years. This was the most exciting adventure. First of all I went alone. I am still amazed that I was so brave to try this one on my own. The company I booked with assured me they would take very good care of me as they had many single people travel with them. I was one of sixteen in our group. I was to land in Arusha, Tanzania, the stopping off point for safaris. But because of circumstances beyond my control (planes!) we had to fly to Kenya then to Tanzania and we lost a day. What a magnificent adventure of the very first magnitude. I saw lions, leopards, cheetahs, elephants, monkeys, giraffes, hippos, rhinos, zebras, wildebeests, cape buffalo, a large variety of birds, wart hogs, hyenas, gazelles, crocodiles, giant termite mounds, a black mamba (highly poisonous snake) tsetse flies and range rovers full of people. I watched as a wiz flew by in the distance it was a cheetah taking down a gazelle. I was in the midst of the wildebeest migration. The total frenzy of the animals was noted when they were at the watering areas. You could hardly see the animals because of the stirred up dust. They stampeded and the day after there were bloated carcasses floating in the water. Water, such a vital necessity for life! The natural world, what an astounding experience!

Very close to Arusha is Mt Kilimanjaro, a dormant volcano, the highest mountain in Africa. We traveled through the Serengeti National Park as well as several other parks. I stayed in tents, not your regular Boy Scout tents. Our showers were large canvas bags with a small shower head and a pull chain. The first couple of days they assumed I had a partner and when they discovered differently they cut my water supply in half. But I didn't realize this until there wasn't enough water to remove the soap. I was so disappointed. The first time I had ever slept in a tent was in the wilds of Africa. I learned a new use for zip lock baggies; they make a good little middle of the night bathroom. Who would have thought! I didn't want to *unzip* that tent for any reason in the middle of the night. We had a Masai guard armed with spears during the night. The last set of tents was the nicest and they were semi-permanent set up for the entire season. We had driven through a prison farm for what seemed like seventy five miles. I never saw a person in that area. I was like a kid asking "are we there yet?" I really didn't like driving through this; my fear was talking to me. Shortly after exiting the prison farm we arrived at our lodgings. I was thinking this is just too close to that prison farm. When I realized we had two armed guards those last two nights, I was a little scared. Especially when one of them carried a "big" gun, a military looking gun! I suspect the people were far more dangerous than the animals.

I also took an early morning hot air balloon ride over the Serengeti. The quiet, the stillness and the sun rise, the beauty of it all. Nature at it's finest. We could see the paths the wildebeest had taken as they congregated to migrate north. We landed with a big bump, the next time I will be more prepared to brace myself for that bump. Then we had a champagne breakfast on the plains; table cloth, silverware, china and bees looking for sweets. It was great fun. What a thrill bees and all. And there was the outdoor loo labeled as such sitting in the middle of the plains of the Serengeti with an exposed side for viewing the scenery. They didn't forget anything.

I got to dance, a jump dance with the Masai ladies. They had beaded collars on. They tried to put one over my head so I would be in the mix. They searched and finally found one with a hole big enough to fit over my head. Smiling. So, I too had a collar.

Africa has two seasons. I would recommend going between the wet and dry seasons. Not choosing one over the other. It was just vast greenness without a soul insight except my group and our land rover. It was very dusty. We did see a few people including a young male who jumped out of his swimming hole nude and was shaking his body parts at us. My eyes were wide and I was saying "Did you see that?" My next thought was amusement in that people are just the same everywhere. I don't think I would like it during the dry season as everything is dead and even dustier. Water becomes the main factor in survival. The animals are found more easily as they are moving continuously in search of water. But I had no problem seeing animals. The guides have this kind of magical quality about finding animals for us to see. Many of the animals are just hanging around close to the road. I think the animals like to show off. Smiling. Or maybe the guides are tossing them food, just a thought. Or maybe they are using their intuition or those little radios "we have lions beside the road here come on over." And sure enough there would be several land rovers jockeying for positions to get the best view for us.

The areas I was exposed to were very primitive compared to my city and my home. There was no infra-structure, no electricity or water supply. It was a personal responsibility to find water and make your fuel even for the coffee plantation we stayed at for two nights. One man we met had a cistern where he put cow dung along with other waste and produced gas for his lighting and stove. He was very proud of his accomplishments and his culture and his independence. He left me with a positive upbeat feeling about him and his life's accomplishments in Africa. This entire trip was a wondrous magical experience.

So in the early morning of our last day we had to get on a plane to take us back to Aursha. I was thinking what else is there I can't even imagine anything else as we had already seen and experienced so much, it was all just overwhelming. Then we flew over an active volcano, it was sending up little puffs, wow! What an adventure into life! Once again I was studying life. Nature is exciting.

I got a "feel" for all the places I visited. Perhaps I was speaking psychic, getting a feeling for each place. It was like I really knew what it was all about. Just a knowing!

We may be coming to the end of an era, the end of the wildlife in Africa. It was almost like saying now is the time to experience this as it won't be around in the future. This African visit will be stored in my consciousness which I think continues on. Well, that was a thought I had and it just might possibly be so. This thought would be based on the idea that we are consciousness and we continue on after this incarnation.

A Most Interesting Life Experience

Or

Discovering the Skeletons in the Closet

I had received some old items from my mother after her transition. She had promised my great aunt she wouldn't throw anything away. Before the age of computers my great aunt did a family genealogy study using an old typewriter and the telephone. What a daunting task that must have been. I can't even imagine. She was so enthusiastic as she collected all the information from my mother's family; there were seven living brothers and sisters, all the spouses and children. My great aunt was the sister of my mother's father. I was a teenager at the time. She would talk about her study and I think I must have been day dreaming because I remember her enthusiasm but not much else. I now understand its importance to her but not then.

I had seen this picture several times when I would go through the papers. But one particular time in June, 2007, I flipped it over and on the back it read, "This was the house I lived in from 1897 to 1908, 11 years. This is Grandma Jones home in Hallsville, Ohio. The civil war troops camped in the front yard on their way south to the war. Great Aunt Florence." Now, Grandma Jones lived from 1827 to 1927. She won a spelling bee when she was ninety-nine. She was very serious and very very strict.

Okay, so, on an impulse I decided to google Hallsville. And the information just came flooding into my computer. It was like a plate being filled with all manner of delightful desserts. I saw some names popup on the screen. Ah, I thought I had this faint recognition of seeing these names before. I was plundering old boxes of things and found seven typed legal pages of information left by my great aunt. The information was all about her life, relatives and early history of the family. She had included some information about family members who had "gifts" I assume intuitive gifts. I was gathering internet information and reading my great aunt's information and things started to come together. The project just grew and grew as more information discovered me.

At one point I made arrangements to go to Hallsville, Ohio. I felt I would find more there like graves and such as that. A cousin of mine had been there and told me there were grave markers. When I got there I found a house I thought was Grandma Jones's. I knew they had given the front corner of the property for a Methodist Church. I felt that was the identifying structure and I could see a house sitting behind the church. I knocked on the door much to my disappointment no one answered. I proceeded to try and get a photo of the house. There were trees in the way I was squatting and stooping and at one time laying in the grass taking pictures of this house. I am grateful I didn't get shot. The really awesome thing! When I got home and started making my genealogy book I looked at the new picture of the house and then the old picture of my aunt's. It was a chilling experience because the new photo was pretty much the same exact angle as the old picture. The same house, just different eras and the trees had grown. It was a most amazing experience. I was thrilled. I thought synchronicity! Hot dog, this was so cool.

As I drove into town I discovered it was a quick blink town. Zip and you were through it. Grandma Jones's father (Buchwalter) founded this small town that was known then as Economy, Ohio. I saw someone walking down the street and asked a question and was directed to a house, once there I explained what I was doing and the man called his mother-in-law. She and I discovered we were distant cousins of our common grandfather who was living and fought during the Revolutionary War. His relatives came over from Alsace-Lorraine to avoid being brought to trial for reading the Bible, they were Protestants. They had to keep the Bible hidden in the barn. They were discovered and warned and they barely escaped the Inquisition officers as they were followed to the ship. The captain covered for them and they were able to make it to the "new county." Can you imagine living through that? It speaks fear to me.

I discovered Grandma Jones mother's ancestors came from Germany and they can be traced back to the original immigrants homesteading in Pennsylvania. He gave property for a church there and it's named after him. Dreisbach was the family name given to the church. A cousin and I went to see the church that has since been rebuilt but still has the old family name. While there we found the grave markers of the man and his wife, the original immigrants from Germany. I think their original house is still standing in Germany.

This whole experience was just like it was all laid out for me to discover. It was very exciting. I had many synchronicities occur. You know when things just come together and they did. It was an awesome adventure. I have printed probably one hundred copies of my genealogy book and they went to extended family members. It contained lineages, many family photos and pictures of grave markers. It was a very interesting exciting adventure. I loved doing this book. It actually started out as a book for my daughter for a Christmas present and it just expanded. Wow, what a journey!

Sometimes I think I was being guided from the other side by my great aunt to finish what she had started. I'm just thinking out loud and smiling.

I have also heard it said; do your genealogy and you will have some ideas about your past lives as we incarnate in groups. One might also be given glimpses of behavioral patterns that tend to run in families. I am in possession of a diary written in 1845 by Grandma Jones's sister Elizabeth (1823-1861). It gives a view of their everyday lives. I have one of the very first photographs ever taken on a mirror of Elizabeth. I had a young man, a former student lift the image from the glass impression to make a current photo of her. The image is actually very good. Elizabeth mentions in the diary waiting for the portrait man to come to town to have her portrait made. I bet it was this picture I have. They probably hadn't coined the word for photograph.

My maternal grandfather taught school in Hallsville before he married my grandmother. He had a room in Penina Pickle's house. She taught my great aunt, she used to talk about Ms. Pickle when I was a child and I always thought what a silly name. When I was there I found her house. The same one my grandfather had roomed in. I found the postal boxes where my great grandfather deposited mail when he was the postmaster.

I have some items from the ancestors I discovered in Ohio. I made the remark: I have something from everyone except, and guess what, I found items belonging to them the very next day. Amazing!

I have all of this information because my great aunt made my mother promise she wouldn't throw any of her things away. All of her stuff provided me with an awesome adventure. I am so grateful to have been able to have this experience. It was almost like I was living with these people while I was studying them it was like reading a novel. I was there with them. Maybe I was one of them in a past life.

This whole project is a good example of the spiritual principle: What we focus on expands. I went from an old photograph, to a genealogy book in a few months. "Bits and Pieces" was an idea whose time had come. I was exposed to Balboa Press in early November 2011at an "I Can Do It" conference and I am just about ready to upload the manuscript today January 8, 2012. It is now March 13, 2012 and I am still not ready. My computer died while writing this book. I think there is far more to writing a book than I first thought. The editing is challenging especially when the old dead computer wasn't working properly. It couldn't possibly be that "I" made any errors. Ha!

It's been a great experience.

One Added Piece

Or

A little sexuality

When I told several people about this idea they asked is there any sex in the book. I just laughed, like I am doing now. I said no. Then I had a second thought or two. Maybe:

Mmm, where to start? Well, we all arrived here as tiny babes because of shhhhhhhh! Yes, sex. Imagine that! I am a result of uh, you know my mom and dad, well, you know. That isn't something we like to think about, is it?

Sexual reproduction perpetuates the species it insures life's future. Those chromosomes containing the master blueprint, DNA, are passed on. Half of the chromosomes come from the mother and the other half from the father. This natural process takes care of continuing the human species on earth. It allows a vehicle for the spirit to experience life here. If spirit is the creator then it has a means through which it is able to create. Spirit is always creating; it is a driving force in the universe. Remember each of us is part of the whole, the whole universe, the ALL that is which is God. Reproduction produces a body in which the spirit resides and creates. Can you just imagine the infinite number of creations spirit can express. God is playing with the universe, his toy, his pleasure, ultimately bringing heaven to earth. What an idea! And as spirit we are helping. I do think some of the time our creations are a little mucky, maybe even a lot mucky but the ultimate goal is to be aware of who we are and our creative abilities and bring heaven to earth. It's all a natural process, God's universe at work.

If there are multiverses, wow what a daunting thought. I just can't even begin to imagine. That almost sounds like fantasy, science fiction. Maybe my story sounds like fiction or science fiction. It's just my experience and the time has come for these ideas to be expressed.

Okie dokie, a little diversion, now down to the serious stuff, let's talk about the sex life of a pine tree. He He! All those little male pollen cones that make everything yellow in the early spring. The bigger female cones we see and are familiar with have the pine seeds. The seed resulted from the pollen uniting with the egg. Interesting? I am laughing because I have a friend I was explaining this to one day, she was so excited to hear (joking here) all about this topic: Sexual reproduction of pine trees. Well, is a very good thing otherwise there would be no more pine trees.

Continuation, a most vital idea for creation *everything* continues onward and that happens because of the sexuality of living things. And we try to have an understanding of these natural processes; cycles of life and of reproduction.

My advice to you is to be careful who you make oxytocin with. It's the bonding molecule made during reproduction and at other times like when nursing a new born. It's just one of the glues that hold people together. Sometimes this chemical glue, oxytocin sets the stage for more than we bargain for. The bond is set and breaking it can be very painful. Sexuality is all part of the journey. It's life.

There is a definite energy exchange during sexual reproduction, a little quantum entanglement, maybe a lot.

Sexuality is definitely a part of life. It has many facets. I'll just let *you* use your imagination to explore the facets.

My Evolution

Well, I believe it was Copernicus using math and his observations that told us the earth was not the center of the universe but the sun was the center of our planetary system. Have we ever heard the term "earthrise?" Before that time the Earth was considered to be the center of everything. What an uproar he caused. How dare he disrupt the prevailing ideas of his time! They were very rude to him, he was treated badly. He was presenting them with a radical new idea and they just couldn't abide it.

Just recently I heard Dr. Bruce Lipton tell us that there is a hierarchy of understanding in the sciences. It was pyramidal in shape with math being the base, just above that physics, then chemistry, then biology and at the very top of the pyramid is psychology.

All of the disciplines rely on those sources below it to explain the topics above it. For example: for biology, one point of understanding is life is matter; I must explore chemistry as all matter is composed of elements; to understand the mechanics of matter physics is needed; to understand both chemistry and physics math is needed as proof.

The questions I asked about life, those who, what, where, when and why questions led me into biology, the science of life. I started studying elementary school music in college and then I had my first freshman biology course. The bells were ringing and it was time to change to biology. I think my limited understanding of math, my fear if it and its difficulty helped place me on a biological path. The two disciplines below biology are all math based. It was the passion for understanding life that landed me in the field of biology. Looking back I was interested in understanding life as seen through the eyes of a biologist. But, I do see there are three disciplines below biology that are the basis for supporting the study and the explanation of biology. Life, which we see, feel, hear, taste and touch results from understanding chemistry, physics and math and how they all work together. Life happens and we are trying to explain it, it's an ongoing process of discovery. But, then there is that which isn't seen, that sixth sense which I believe can be explained using math, physics and chemistry. Technology and experimental design are definitely limiting factors in understanding there really is a sixth sense. The sixth sense is a part of life. Life is what we experience and sometimes it seems just a little bit strange. Or so it would seem based on society's current understanding about life and how things work. It's a "prove" it attitude. Sometimes the proof comes in experiences like mine. A personal experience! How would you develop an experimental design for my experience?

So I am grasping the hugeness of the planetary system and our position in the Galaxy. Then I got a touch of Quantum mechanics (we are all energy) and then I got this view of Multiverses. There is mathematical support for multi-universes. So how do we find them? That's a huge question. Ha! Obviously something had to happen before the big bang to produce our universe. Oh, it just goes on and on and now multi-verses too. So, I stop here to just say infinite love and gratitude for all that is understood, that which is misunderstood and that which is yet to be discovered, because sooner or later the misunderstandings become understandings. It's the drive behind understanding that keeps us moving forward. It's all very overwhelming. These are huge concepts to grasp. Infinity, there's more than we could possibly dream. The physicists tell us in another universe the probability of another me is highly likely. Wow, another me who has experienced and mastered other ideas and concepts I am still struggling with. There is a man that teaches quantum jumping. He says in consciousness you can jump into another reality where you have mastered an idea or talent that you don't know here. Then you can bring it back and experience it here.

I have had many of my who, what, when, where and why questions answered and then more questions follow. Whew, and the beat goes on throughout infinity and beyond. I am glad because at one point in time I so longed to know what 6000 years ahead would be like and some how I think I will know.

The bottom line, I am wishing infinite love and gratitude for a life that has been challenging. It has lead me down a path covered with prickles, beauty and multi-experiences. I am an explorer, obviously delving into the mix of it all. My searching has all been in the name of creating a lovelier, nicer reality. Only recently have I become consciously aware of this idea, to have the intention to create a better reality for myself. How does one do that? For me, first I had to understand who, what, when, where and maybe a why. Then I discovered I was part of the "all that is" the one. I was a tiny piece of the whole big thing. Wow! How powerful is that. I have infinite love and gratitude for discovering that and that I help co-create this life. Another wow! I know some of what life (biology and experience) is all about and I find myself in a most fortunate place and am thankful for all I have learned. My focus on science and spirituality became my evolution by understanding first of all who I am and then how I co-create my reality. I also discovered some of the time I am not so keen on the reality I have created. When I become aware I can change it to lovelier and nicer. It's a matter of consciousness.

This book, "Bits & Pieces" is about my evolution, in fact ever day is adding to who I am and how I see my world. How fortunate am I to have arrived at this understanding at this point in time. I am just so passionate about this. It's a very good place to be especially without the anxiety and panic.

I wish to extend a word of thanks to Dr. Wayne Dyer for his contributions to all of us. The power of intention ignited a fire within and it has been a force pushing me onward.

Some God Notes

Or

How I Think Things Work

My personal experiences have led me to believe that all is God and we are in each others lives to allow our own personal growth and to understand more about who we are. It is my *personal relationship* with the Universe, God; actually I can attach any name I wish to it. But it's the recognition that I am part of the *All* that is and that I can live the spiritual principles that Jesus taught, and that I am finding God within, and that I understand these things. But my understanding is not in the traditional generic brand of religion or of our society's ideals. It gives me goose bumps to have this understanding. I must assume responsibility for me, my thoughts, and my words. God is not sitting out there meting out blessings if I am good enough or punishments if I am really bad. It might just be me making a karmic adventure in the sea of God. Life times of happenings within the laws of the universe. The laws are always working as we ride the wave co-creating with love or any other emotion and it's always returned in kind.

If I want to be a victim then I can always say it was out there, not me that created this. The "Word" is important. It's vibratory! It is what is expanded upon to create our realities. The words make up our thought patterns, aware or unaware we are creating our reality.

Just look around, take in what you see, Does it all belong to you? The Universe is giving us what we want it doesn't tell us no only yes.

There is not an arm chair man sitting "out there" that is judging, reprimanding, dishing out punishments and condemning those to the lost unforgiven place. We are the ones doing this not God. We have to beg no one for blessings. We just have to wake up, become aware that it's us, you and I; we are the co-creators of what we see around us. We create our blessings as we *believe* it to be so. Nature is gracious in its bounty; it's here for us to use "wisely." I question our decisions about our natural environment; probably most of them aren't very wise.

Ask and it is given to the measure of our belief. When we ask, sit back and observe, smell the roses and really believe, we know our idea will bear fruit. That doesn't mean we don't have to roll up our sleeves. The most wonderful fun filled part is watching it come about. The Universe can surprise us in so many ways. Now the reality for me is, this is happening all the time, we are unconscious or we are conscious. Some of us are much better at this than others are just naturally. The principles are right here before us for the learning! They are universal laws. They are found in the world's major religions. There are common threads that run through all of the great religions. Many have discovered them, like Ernest Holmes for one. Mystics know how things work; they understand the workings of the universal laws. Jesus was the ultimate master. We are on an evolutionary path to improve our human species. Lift up life into a better place as we become more aware and more conscious of our creative abilities. It's rather an exciting journey.

I have a biology back ground, I taught biology in high school for thirty years and in the last few years have been especially focused on spirituality also. For me my blended science and spirituality is one in the same. Nature is God expressing itself. The natural working of the Universe is God expressing itself. My life, all my experiences have served me well to be in the place I am today. My present choice of spiritual growth comes from Ernest Holmes who wrote the book "Science of Mind."

The Universe is abundant, and willing to give us what we ask for. Remember we are a piece of the whole, a tiny fragment of God because God is all that is and I am part of that. I am one with the All that is. And it is all energy. I am energy that has assumed a particular form and that form is able to observe itself and have some understanding of how things work. In the creative process there was the word. I need to choose my words wisely. When I first came upon this concept of the importance of my words I was overwhelmed. I discovered that much of my thinking was so negative. I listen to the words coming from my lips and the thoughts racing through my mind and it helps to enlighten me about my core beliefs. My core beliefs can be difficult to pinpoint as they come from the programing I received early in my life, zero to about six years. I am the observer. Once I am aware, then I am able to change those words to more positive affirmations. Being present in the moment allows me to catch that negativity bubbling up from my years of programming. Our brains are like computers tucking away so many billions of bits of information that frame who we are at this moment. All the positive and the negative and all the teachings we have absorbed. Whew! Let's clean house. It's about feeling more joy and happiness and being more peaceful, making heaven on earth. It's about changing those yucky things to feel good things. Life is awesome!

Ideas Worth Repeating

Or

Things I Like to Think About

Karma is neither good nor bad, but simply a balancing act which occurs over multiple lifetimes. We define the quality of the karma by making a judgment calling it good or bad.

Karma is working, even if we aren't aware. As we sow so shall we reap. It's a spiritual principle and one of Newton's laws.

Fractal geometry is the geometry of patterns, patterns that are repeatable in the universe. They are reflected in life forms. They are derived from a mathematical calculation that can be added back to itself or subtracted from the original equation to produce a pattern. The patterns are beautiful designs. Some crop circles are fractals, derived from mathematical equation. I believe our bodies are based on fractal geometry. Is it the geometry of life? Gregg Braden has helped me understand this topic.

How many experiences could we create on this planet earth I believe infinite numbers. This is the planet of opposites. How can we know one unless we have experienced the other? The light and dark. The yen and yang. The love and hate. I'm sure you can think of more opposites. The opposites allow for experiences and understandings. Once we understand our unity with the one the opposites are no longer necessary teachers.

A universal principle: What we focus on expands.

The result: In the name of the Father, the Son and the Holy Spirit. As it is above so below, from God to the Son, through love do we find heaven on earth and the gift of Spirit. This is an evolvement in progress. Always moving forward!

The Angel Gabriel says look for joyful synchronicities in every day life. I think we miss most of them. In fact I am sure I miss many of them. So I am looking forward to experiencing joyful, playful daily synchronicities that reveal to me spirit's dance in my life.

While I was writing the story about not smoking and typed in the date August 12, 1992; I walked away from the computer and thought oh my goodness another significant event happened August 12, 2011. The date I discovered my ex-husband was still with me even though he had made his transition in '08. In '08 I considered it his death. Now it's his transition. What a transformation. I had a rush of goose bumps. For me goose bumps are a sign of resonance with spirit. Is this synchronistic? Just sayin.

Who are my change agents, my inertia busters, my soul mates? They are the people who challenge me as I discover my ability to respond to them lovingly and not in a negative way. They provide me with a gift of love. As Neale Donald Walsch says, "Life begins at the end of your comfort zone."

Kahlil Gibran says in "The Prophet" that our children don't really belong to us but come through us wanting to express life. We may give them love but we can't give them our thoughts, as much as that maybe our desire. Their souls are a generation ahead and are moving beyond us into the future. Life goes forward not backwards. We provided them with an entrance to life. It is theirs to cherish and discover and experience as it was ours.

What is it about human nature, we see our self as the center of the hub and we want others to merge with us and be right there in that hub of same thinking. Perhaps that is what we call our experience of separateness and we keep trying to complete it by trying to draw them all into our hub.

Every person in your life is there because you have drawn them to you with your vibrational frequency. How you respond is up to you.

What you put out there and focus on expands. If you push forth with an idea giving it energy with a pinch of passion it will come to fruition.

Life is spirit experiencing human form. When it gets to worn it transforms and returns again later for a new life. Sometimes it may leave early or it seems to us it's leaving to early. It maybe that is exactly as it is supposed to be.

This planet has infinite numbers of possibilities for experiencing whatever you wish.

Choices, choices, choices, too many choices are sometimes confusing.

The universe (uni = one) may actually be multi-verses.

Constructive criticism is there such a thing. An oxymoron perhaps, can criticism a spoken or written disproval really be constructive? Perhaps constructive feedback might be a better term.

When someone repeatedly corrects you, are you going to share who you are with them?

Look around you; everything is there because you arranged for it to be there in some manner or form. My intention becomes my creation, my outward creation even my inner creation. I have created my reality. I am the one responsible. Now looking inward I have words and thoughts that create emotional feelings. Patterns are repeating themself through my life. This is my inward creation. My body, my circumstances, I provide it all with what I feed it. All the molecules I consume become me. All the words I feed it are me. My life is totally my creation out there as well as within. Wow!

All societies, cultures in the world and our technology are there because we created it. This is our world we made it so. Did it all just happen? Not! We need to awaken!

Sin means to miss the mark. So I fall short then I try again. Unfortunately there has been so much focus on sin, oh we are so worthless, so bad, so unworthy. Our inner conflicted core beliefs are that we are worthless sinners, just junk. Sin can be used to control people. This doesn't make sense to me. I am not "that" but I have experienced those feelings based on the current underlying concepts in our culture. We learn this very early, when we are so young, it is stored away and effects behavior and our ability to create healthy lives. We must become aware and change the thought process to the proper definition of sin. If I have no self-worth I am not going to make much of my creation as I ruminate on my unworthiness. I think this misunderstood idea of sin and it's obsession in our world is not healthy. Its consciousness evolution, we are so much more than we have been lead to believe. Ideas change and society changes. It's time for change.

I have an idea, where did it come from? I try to see where it fits in my frame of reference (the sum total of my experiences). I might think it over and sit down at the keyboard. Oh, what a wonder these computers. The process continues the brain sends the idea, a message, to my fingers, tap, tap dancing over the keys, up pop the symbols, the words. Then I send the ideas to my friend. The light reflects off of those little symbols. Her eyes see the light energy; her brain turns the symbols into an idea (left brain) or picture (right brain). Instantly, she reacts from her frame of reference and responds with thought or word and emotion. Just one of the ways we communicate and express what and how we experience the world. Pretty cool process. The wonder of it all!

I have experienced the evolution of writing technology. With a pencil in hand I wrote, and then I discovered a typewriter. Now I use this marvelous instrument called a computer. And now the internet has the capability of connecting me to everyone, literally worldwide.

My experiences are so strange according to "polite" society. I told my counselor one day I was not your typical female she agreed but she said I was very interesting. I liked that. If I can make anyone's life easier, help them find their path, then so be it. And most of all provide a better understanding about anxiety/panic that in some cases it might be an energy entanglement issue. Either way I have given something to the world.

During my early years I was involved with traditional earth religions. I played for the services in a Presbyterian church for about 15 years. I have listened to many sermons. I read the Bible. I organized a summer day camp program for mentally challenged children. But my real understanding of spirituality came from metaphysical experiences. Listening to my intuition and the door cracking open for understanding the psychic side of reality has given me my experience of knowing. It has been my own personal journey nothing anyone could give me but through my interacting with them I have understanding about me. "Iam."

A Significant Ceremony

Or

Lighting the Flames of Faith

I borrowed this from the Spiritual Center I go to it's a ceremony that is held monthly. I find it to be so significant in peace making and understanding that ALL is part of God. It is performed to promote the universal consciousness of life, which acknowledges that all peoples and all faiths, all sentient beings, come from the One Great Universal Presence, which we call Spirit. Fundamental to this truth is the unifying nature of all religious thought and experience which we honor by lighting a candle for each discipline.

The first candle is for the Tao, honoring the universal path of harmony and equilibrium, the natural way.

The second we light for the Shamanic Traditions, honoring the beliefs and practices of all indigenous peoples, the way of primal spirituality.

The third is for Hinduism, honoring the path of knowledge, action and devotion.

The fourth candle is lit for Judaism, honoring the ethical path of living by sacred law.

The fifth candle is for all forms of Buddhism, honoring The Four Noble Truths and the path of compassion.

The sixth candle is lit for all forms of Christianity, honoring the Christ Consciousness as the path of love.

The seventh is for all forms of Islam, honoring the path of submission to the will of God as the highest calling.

The eighth candle is for the universal religion of Baha'i, honoring the path of unity in all religions and peace.

We light the ninth candle for all forms of New Thought, honoring the metaphysical path of mental healing through the practice of universal spiritual principles.

The last candle is lit for healing, it is the healing candle. Please take a moment to silently put the name of someone you wish to have the experience of the healing flame of God's eternal love.

For me this is such a profound moment there is a presence of unity of all peoples, honoring all religions. We are all one there are many paths.

In Conclusion

Or

What's In My God Box?

Well, let's see. I think I have stated how I had to rearrange my thinking. That is all the beliefs that I have stored in the file under God. I call this my God box. Today, in the stillness of the early morn I had my conclusion thought out. It's a fine place to be, listening and thinking. Wow, I like the ideas, especially the ideas that I feel are coming from my connection to the ALL that is. My journey has brought me to a place, thank goodness, that I am not feeling all of that painful turmoil. That place where I was wasting my thinking time ruminating, churning or mulling over past incidences or even current happenings.

Many times as stated in "Bit & Pieces" I have felt the pangs of internal discomfort, sometimes severe discomfort. You know that "owiee yuck" feeling that sweeps over me when I feel threatened in some way, or insulted. It's an opportunity for me to learn more about who I am. Not smack them over the head with a dead chicken which might just be my initial thought. But then I remember I am a work in progress and there is a law that says what I put out there will return to me. Duh, I maybe a blonde but I have this one understood. That is everything I put out there comes back to me! It's a law, a natural working of a law of the universe. I am correcting all the time, peeling the onion, getting clearer. And the payoff is having fewer of those "owiee yuck" feelings. Yes, more peace more joy more happiness, finding the heaven within.

The collective consciousness is all those beliefs that we as humans hold to be the absolute truth about everything that is, including God. Everything is energy. Thoughts are energy. Remember when I told the story about the "Dr. Who" shows being received back on earth after thirty years of moving away from earth. Energy happening. If thoughts aren't energy why pray? What else might they be?

Well, I think the God box of the collective consciousness has many facets. The one I am most familiar with is the Santa Claus God. There is much Santa Clause God in the collective consciousness of the human race. If I pray enough, and I'm good enough, and I smile enough, and I go to church enough then I just might get my request. Or I might get the judgments and the punishments meted out as warranted. And I have to say there were many times I was feeling and thinking what have I done to have "this or that" particular experience. That's what I think is a childlike God concept. As I grew and matured a little I discovered there isn't anyone out there making all of those declarations. It's me making the judgments and correcting the other person's path by swinging the dead chicken fixing them, putting *them* on the corrected path. Oh, mercy! Did I create my world based on the Santa Clause God concept? I believe I did. It's my path, It's me, energy is everything, God is all that is, I am in unity with God, that God box had to be dissembled, rearranged and rebuilt. I am finding my ancestry, my origins with God an awesome thing. I am responsible.

Where do science and spirituality come together, Einstein's equation about energy enhances my beliefs about who I am and what I come from and how it happens. When I incorporated the newest science, the quantumness of life, into my frame of reference on what makes things work, light bulbs, ah! moments, come on for me. God is nature and science explains nature and I am part of nature. Understanding how I currently believe my God works within me and for me becomes clearer with science. Having the ODE (other dimension experience) experience confirms for me there is a transition to another place and that would be energy is transformed. This is my God concept not yours. You can choose to believe whatever works for you. If I still wanted a flat world then I have that choice. I am finding that for me all of this is biblical, it's just more mature and redefined with my shifted view, a huge shift in consciousness. I have read the Bible several times but I just now understand it. It was a believing issue for me. This is a new way for me to look at the "ALL" that is. Is this a New Age? The Age of Aquarius? The new dawn? Is that really what 2012 is all about? The new age is dawning and I think it has its roots in the movements of planets, suns and galaxies in our universe. Our earth's place in space relative to the galaxy and it's the energy we are being exposed to that is causing many of the changes we are and have been experiencing. The Mayan's knew this. But how do you tell future generations? It's like putting pieces of a puzzle together. Everything is always cycling. If the cycles are thousands of years, how do we, today, know that? Maybe science! We are dutifully at work trying to discover the answers. The clues are here. Discovery, but open-mindedness with a touch of reserve is a must! How many fears are we holding onto about anything new? That is where the attacks come from, the fear! Are we being controlled by fear or love? Who is doing the controlling, of course "I am." How many of us are truly aware of what we are feeling, who is feeling that fear of course "I am." The only other thing is love. Have you and I heard "God is love?"

Concepts can now be rearranged and redefined and rebuilt to fit in my new God box. My God box needs to reflect more peace, joy, happiness and my goodness play. So I have to be more peace, joy and happiness and play. Today I saw something that said just get rid of the "box," and I think that's a great idea. I have set the intention to have no box, to be discerning and to know when I am experiencing truth.

We are awash in a sea of air. Can we see it, no but it's life affirming. Marine animals are in a sea of water, most likely they don't know that but it's life affirming. Perhaps the marine mammals know where they are. From our perspective we can see the water. We are awash in a universe so vast it's beyond my imagination. We are awash in God, it's always there. How do we interact with this energy I am going to call God. The Bible tells us how. The Bible is experiential. The physicists tell us there is this energy field that is everywhere. I can't see it can you? Can we influence it? I think so. Maybe I can communicate with it using my intuition, prayer. Jesus told us we communicate with this field using love. We have called it God because it is so much larger than life itself. And we just don't understand so much of the natural functions of nature at this point in time. Science is very young, only about 300 years old. God is nature it's ALL that is. How are we limiting God with our own thinking? As Louise Hay says tell yourself you love you each day. First and foremost we need to love ourselves. Jesus said you can do much more than me. I think we interact with this vast field with our words and thoughts and emotions. It's just a natural happening. We receive what we ask for. How many words flip through our brain daily? The words when repeated with emotion, love or hate, are given power. This is how we are creating. Not just now and then but always! As Henry Ford says if you think you can, you can. If you think you can't that is true also. As a man thinks so he is.

My journey has resulted in more harmony in my life. Literally, I have processed negative energy and deleted much of it, refined and redefined so that I am in a place that is so much closer to heaven than I was. Is this called bringing heaven to earth? I am vibrating at a lighter frequency and sometimes I think I can feel the vibrations. Thank goodness this is so. I am clearer, cleaner and lighter. I am filled with gratitude for my gift of knowing. I am so blessed to have the anxiety gone. The amazing weirdness of it all! What a *wow* journey, I am having goose bumps while writing this. They told me in "The Wizard of Oz" how things were. Oh wow, clicking my heels together as I continue walking down the yellow brick road to find the wizard. I believe I have already found him. Just smiling!

Afterwards

I really can't say what happened. Perhaps there were several things working to cause the anxiety: my ex-husband's presence; the unrequited love; the unresolved baggage of a life time; making decisions about my mentally challenged adult child. Anyone or all of these can produce an emotional storm.

My mentally challenged daughter by the way is doing beautifully living on her own in a retirement complex. Just forty years ago we secluded people with such problems because they scared us. There is a twenty four/seven managerial staff. There is a lady that comes and checks on her so many hours per week, a huge blessing for me. She now has another best friend besides me. She is interacting nicely with the older people. It's like having lots of grandmas. We met someone in the grocery store the other day a young woman came up and gave her a hug. She then explained to me how my daughter had helped her grandma when she moved into the apartment complex; she said my daughter was her grandma's first best friend. She was telling her how grateful she was for her companionship with her grandma.

She works in a sheltered workshop which she has done since she graduated from school. The sheltered workshop has a bus and she is transported daily. She will be fifty in October. There was much anxiety about this being a good thing for her, her living on her own. After being there over two years she told me recently that it was the best thing for her living there with her dog Maxine.

I can see some changes in her level of maturity as she is now more responsible for herself. I'm not directing her in ever move and doing the mother nagging thing. I am aware of my idea of the way things are supposed to be for her which isn't always the best especially when I am doing the nagging thing. She has had some growth experiences that have amused me. She decided to take off Fridays and Mondays from work just getting a couple of extra vacation days. After about 6 of her days off, I got a call from her supervisor telling me she hadn't been there and then told me the dates, I discovered the pattern. She had made some decisions about how to live her life; I was excited about that, maybe not the best decisions. But, that's part of being responsible for oneself. She is having the opportunity to have that experience.

She doesn't read but she recognizes every day common words like Wal-Mart. She is just learning about money. So no matter what the age even if it's very slowly we are all on a learning path. We were in the bookstore the other day and she was looking for a book about making change and money. We didn't find one but will continue to look. She knows how to work the microwave. She knows how to keep her clothes clean. Sometime she amazes me with what she knows. But one of the things we don't agree on is I am very neat and things are in place and I don't have much clutter around. She is the opposite which is a very good reason for her to have her own space.

She can be very sweet and caring. She might not have the intellectual abilities as the so called "norm." What she does have is the same emotions as we all have. She is at a disadvantage in that she just reacts and has a limited ability to process the emotion and be logical. But she is also here to learn and teach and grow and become clear. She too is spirit having an earth experience. Whew, what a trip.

I have another daughter who is most capable, very intelligent and able to manage her own life. She is married and they have two lovely young ladies, my granddaughters. They are in their teens and are highly functioning successful young people. I attribute their success to their parent's great parenting skills and my granddaughters who have their own unique personalities. My biggest regret is they haven't lived closer to me. But they know me and for that I am grateful.

So I have no idea what was happening to me with the anxiety. It was like being in the valley of the shadow of death. I have throughout my life repeated the 23 Psalm numerous times, understanding it better with each successive repeating. It has carried me through many disasters. I love the still waters part and the restores my soul. Perhaps it was what they call the dark night of the soul, that anxiety. The problem is it wasn't just one night. Many a time I thought I was going to die from the symptoms I was having. Perhaps it was a culmination of all the experiences in my life and I hit a place of no longer being able to handle it but I was still functioning, I have to say with much tension. Today is a brighter time. I still struggle with circumstances but I process them faster than I used to. It's like having a clearing of the negative energy I was holding in my energy field and I am now addressing current happenings and not being driven by old issues. I am so very grateful.

One of the major healing factors for me is my introduction to Ernest Holmes work. He spent his early years gathering and synthesizing to produce his final ideas about how things work. He searched the works of the great religions and studied Emerson and Thomas Troward. His studies culminated in the "Science of Mind" text. Essentially he is saying that there is a universal mind, intelligence, God, source field or any other name you wish to call it. We are all interacting with it all the time. There is a language, the words we use to access and interact with God. We are part of God, but first we must understand this. We go within to find our own divinity. Jesus came to teach us how to do this. It is our purpose to go to the father, God, the universal mind, the source field asking that it be so. There are certain spiritual laws we must work with to see the fruits of our intention. When this happens we experience so called miracles. No miracles just the universal laws working and our ability to see. That is how we get heaven on earth.

Since we are all pieces parts once we find our divinity it leads the way for others to do the same. It becomes a domino effect. Remember it's all energy. And when we collectively have this idea of knowing who we are we are closer to experiencing heaven on earth. I am a work in progress. We are evolving humanity each of us doing our part. By doing so, we positively effect the collective consciousness of humanity. Perhaps that was my purpose for this visit, my intent to positively affect the collective consciousness of humanity. The rest has been the journey getting me to this moment.

As I was reviewing my daily reading the day I composed this bit I found: "Everyone who is destined to have a spiritual transformation comes to the journey with a wound as big as God. There are few people who become advanced mystics because they simply feel happy on Sunday afternoon." Andrew Harvey. Not saying I am a mystic. Just saying that discomfort leads to comfort and the wounded become whole.

Namaste, Janet Connell, April 2, 2012

About the Author

Janet Southall Connell grew up in Mobile AL. Her interest as of late has been about science and spirituality. She is an explorer. This book is about extraordinary experiences that have led her to her present understanding of "how things work." Her formal education consisted of a Bachelor's degree in biology education, a Master's degree in counselor education and master's level work in biology from the University of South Alabama. She taught science mainly biology in the Mobile County Schools for thirty years in one capacity or another. She currently resides in a small community across the bay from Mobile which she considers to be a little piece of heaven. Her immediate family consists of two daughters, a son-in-law and two granddaughters. She has a musical background and has been singing in a community chorale for about ten years. She has painted with oils and watercolors. She enjoys the mentally challenging card game of bridge. She has just discovered that writing a book can be fun. She has thought of getting a dog, maybe one day.